The Leaven of Laughter
for
Lent and Easter
by
James E. Atwood

Illustrations by Pat McGeachy

Illustrations by Pat McGeachy

Note for Librarians: A cataloguing record for this book is available from
Library and Archives Canada at www.collectionscanada.ca/amicus/index-e.html
ISBN 1-4120-8076-2

PUBLISHING™

Offices in Canada, USA, Ireland and UK

Book sales for North America and international:
Trafford Publishing, 6E–2333 Government St.,
Victoria, BC V8T 4P4 CANADA
phone 250 383 6864 (toll-free 1 888 232 4444)
fax 250 383 6804; email to orders@trafford.com
Book sales in Europe:
Trafford Publishing (UK) Limited, 9 Park End Street, 2nd Floor
Oxford, UK OX1 1HH UNITED KINGDOM
phone 44 (0)1865 722 113 (local rate 0845 230 9601)
facsimile 44 (0)1865 722 868; info.uk@trafford.com
Order online at:
trafford.com/05-3074
10 9 8 7 6 5 4 3 2

INTRODUCTION

The Leaven of Laughter has hundreds of humorous quotes and provocative anecdotes for busy church professionals and volunteers. I know from many years of personal experience how demanding it is to work in the faith community. Someone likened it to being a dog at a whistler's convention.

It's a rewarding but a difficult assignment to be all things to all people at all times. Nevertheless, other's expectations pale before those we place on ourselves to deliver sermons or lead classes week in and week out which would inspire, comfort, and challenge our hearers. And we only get twenty minutes to "wake the dead."

The book is organized around 44 themes which are intrinsic to the Lenten and Easter Seasons. The book is testimony that one of the best tools to keep "the saints" awake and focused is the thoughtful use of humor in one's sermons or presentations. Over and over, I have watched people refocus and listen more intently after hearing a humorous remark. Humor has the power to:

- Puncture human pompousness and pride
- Combat hypocrisy
- Expose ignorance or bad decisions
- Enable an audience to psychologically identify with the speaker
- Diffuse explosive situations and help resolve conflicts
- Build bridges of understanding and communication
- Release us from the crushing seriousness of life
- Increase concentration and listening capacity
- Heal broken spirits
- Reduce our fears
- Open us up to hear and accept new ideas
- Capture the attention of children and youth

It gives me joy to share *The Leaven of Laughter* with those who will, in turn, share its treasures with others as they tell God's good news with a twinkle in their eye.

~

ACKNOWLEDGEMENTS

Literally thousands of people are responsible for this book. I'm indebted to the famous and infamous, to celebrated authors and writers of graffiti. I'm grateful to wise men and women and to simple folk who lifted my spirits with a bumper sticker. Thanks to those legions of story tellers from the dawn of recorded history to those who use the internet today to share laughter and truth. And let's all be grateful to the God who laughs at us (Psalm 2) and puts laughter in our mouths. (Psalm 126:2)

I give special thanks to my wife, Roxana, who for almost half a century has graciously listened to "my stories" and *seldom* replied, "I've heard that one before." What a gift! Both of us are grateful for the many hours of laughter we have shared with our children, Mebane and David, who have given us such joy, and for whom laughter is always an integral part of their day.

I particularly appreciate Dr. Martin Marty, editor of the journal, "Context"; Dr. Ernest Campbell and his *"Notebook"*; and the editors of "The Presbyterian Outlook". A special appreciation, also, to Dr. William Sloane Coffin, Ross Phares, and David MacLellan, whose wit and wisdom I have used extensively.

I'm ever grateful to Bill Marlowe who acquainted me with the amazing possibilities of the computer and helped me organize the first drafts of my material.

I am forever grateful to my friend, June Hess, who sensed immediately the potential of this book for the faith community and went to work with energy, intelligence, imagination, and love to help me organize it in its final form. My extra special thanks to my colleague, collaborator, and illustrator extraordinaire, the Rev. Pat McGeachy, in whose creative drawings I see not only myself, but the entire human family.

In compiling and editing this book, I have been diligent to give credit when I knew to whom credit was due. A caveat is in order. I have in my files virtually the same quotation credited to Thomas Jefferson, John Curran, Patrick Henry, Wendell Phillips, and *perhaps* a few more. When one works with humor, who should be credited is an even trickier proposition. Think—"Have you heard the one about…?" Now—add material shared over the internet--and answering the question, "Whose story is it?" becomes a far from exact science. I did the best I could.

The reader will find many anonymous quotes for which I make no apology. But, as one unknown person said, "If it is the truth, what does it matter who said it first?" Terence, the Roman author of comedies, (190-159 BCE), reminded us thousands of years ago that "Nothing has yet been said that's not been said before." Like any modern day net surfer, Terence may not have known where all the funny stories came from, but he *was* aware that humor as well as profound wisdom, belong to everyone and a good laugh or a wise insight should be shared as widely as possible.

~

CONTENTS

for Roxana

BAPTISM

~

His big sister was excited at the prospect of her five year old brother's baptism but after several weeks had elapsed, she complained to her mom. "I am very disappointed in Peter's baptism. I really thought he'd act better, but I haven't seen any change at all."

~

After her little sister was baptized, a child met her minister at the door and inquired, "Tell me some more about the holy goat."

~

A minister, about to baptize a young girl in a North Carolina river, told her he was going to wash all her sins away. "My goodness," she giggled, "in that itty bitty ol' crick?"

~

In the early church, the unbaptized never joined in intercessory prayer for others. Praying and service on another's behalf were the duties of the baptized. The baptized were the voices reminding God of the poor, and the church, and the troubles of the world. It was practically a job description. —*Gabe Huck, Triduum.*

~

Children are curious about baptism. One little boy in my church put his hand in the water, sloshed it around and asked, "What's going on here? Is this real water?"

~

In baptism parents promise to raise their children in the Christian faith in the same way that they are going to offer them nutritional foods. The day may come when the child will say, "I don't want to eat that." But good parents always start with good nutrition. —*Andre Dubus.*

The Church was party to the scandal of slavery by refusing baptism for slaves. Clergy were often instructed, "Don't baptize my slaves. Baptism makes them proud, and not such good servants."

~

How beautiful will be the day when all the baptized understand that their work, their job, is a priestly work: that, just as I celebrate Mass at the altar, so each carpenter celebrates Mass at the workbench—each metalworker—each professional—each doctor with the scalpel—each market woman at her stand—are performing a priestly office! How many cabdrivers I know listen to this message there in their cabs; you are a priest at the wheel, my friend, if you work with honesty, consecrating that taxi of yours to God, bearing a message of peace and love to the passengers who ride in your cab. —*Bishop Oscar Romero.*

~

Novelist Kurt Vonnegut, Jr., portrays a secular christening scene in one of his novels: "Hello Babies. Welcome to earth. It's round and wet and crowded. At the outside, Babies, you've got about a hundred years here. There's only one rule that I know of, Babies. Damn it, you've got to be kind!"

~

The latest fad is Hot Tub Baptism in California. At least that is the scene for the New Song Church in Covina, California. Their slogan is, "The flock that likes to rock." —*"Religious News".*

~

A veterinarian reports: A client brought a litter of golden retriever puppies to my veterinary clinic for inoculations and worming. As the look-alike pups squirmed over and under one another in their box, I realized it would be difficult to tell the treated ones from the rest. I turned on the water faucet, wet my fingers, and moistened each dog's head when I had finished. After the fourth puppy, I noticed my hitherto talkative client had grown silent. As I sprinkled the last pup's head, the woman leaned forward and whispered, "I didn't know they had to be baptized."—*"Veterinarian Magazine".*

~

A Presbyterian and a Baptist minister were having their usual argument about baptism: Presbyterian: *Would I be baptized, if I got into the water up to my armpits?*
> Baptist: *Nope!*
> Presbyterian: *Then--how about up to my nose?*
> Baptist: *No...*
> Presbyterian: *Well—how about just below my hairline?*
> Baptist: *Still—nope!*
> Presbyterian: *See--that's what I've been telling you all along!*
> *It's what's up top that counts!*

~

An Englishman was asked by the minister, "What are the Christian names of your twin daughters?" The poor fellow was so nervous, he responded, "Steak and Kidney." The wife, made the correction,"No, it's Kate and Sydney."

—*David MacLennan, Church Chuckles.*

The building inspector was escorted throughout the church facility by the new Baptist preacher. He casually asked, "Do you have a sprinkler system in this church? The young preacher was indignant, "This *is* a Baptist Church, sir."

~

There have been 380,000 holocaust victims posthumously baptized into the Mormon Church without their families' permission. *—"Harpers' Bazaar," (09-1995).*

~

The Methodist owner of the fish market advertised a special on "Baptist Fish." He put them on ice outside on a stand on the sidewalk. When a customer said, "They don't smell very good," the owner replied, "That's why we call them *Baptist Fish.* They spoil as soon as they're taken out of the water."

~

In a portion of the old West the early settlers tried to convert the Indians to the Baptist, Methodist and Friends communities. Two Indians were overheard discussing them. "Just what is the difference between them?" asked one. The other replied, "Big wash, little wash, no wash." *—Anonymous.*

~

A small Baptist congregation in Kansas had a baptism in the river on a cold March morning. There was only one convert to be baptized. After the preacher had put him under, someone asked him, "Is the water cold?" Summoning all his macho spirit, he replied, "Oh, no." One of the Deacons said, "Dip him again, Preacher. He's lyin."

~

We preach this way because we wish to shake our baptized people out of the habits that threaten to make them practically baptized pagans, idolaters of their money and power. What sort of baptized persons are these? Those who want to bear the mark of the Spirit and the fire that Christ baptizes with must take the risk of renouncing everything and seeking only God's reign and justice.

—Bishop Oscar Romero.

~

The man was a real sinner but, every time there was a revival in town, he'd attend and get religion and ask to be baptized, again. After he had been baptized five or six times, the preacher put him under the water, raised him up and said, "You've been baptized so often in this river that the fish know you by name."

~

When an old reprobate was baptized, the preacher said to him, "John, all your sins—and they are many—have been washed away in this river, just as you can see the currents going downstream. John replied, "God help the fish."*—Ben L. Rose.*

~

The country boy was asked if he believed in infant baptism. "Believe in it?" he asked. "Hell, I've seen it."

When you confess your faith in Jesus Christ and are baptized, draw strength from the words you spoke and be watchful. Your adversary, the devil, prowls like a roaring lion, seeking whom he may devour. Formerly death was powerful and could devour.; but in the bath of the new birth, God has dried all the tears from every face. Never again shall you weep; you shall always be on holiday, for you have put on the garment of salvation.

—Cyril of Jerusalem, 4th C.

~

As a child, Harris Kirk,* watched the minister baptize a baby boy. He had never seen that done before, so he inquired of his mother what it meant. She said "When the minister baptizes a baby, it means that he is God's boy." Harris was quiet for a moment and then said, "Then I'm God's boy too." His mother said, "Yes, you are God's boy too." Harris Kirk said he never forgot what it meant for him to know that he was not only a boy, but God's boy, dedicated to God from his youth.

Harris Kirk was Pastor of First Presbyterian Church, Baltimore, MD.

~

The poet, Samuel Coleridge, tells of a conversation he had with a friend who felt it unfair to influence a child's mind by inculcating any opinions, especially on religious matters, before the child was able to choose for himself. "I showed him my garden," said Coleridge, "and told him it was my botanical garden." His friend didn't understand, pointing out that the garden was full of weeds. "Oh," said Coleridge, "That's only because it has not yet come to the age of discretion and choice. The weeds, you see, have taken the liberty to grow and I thought it unfair of me to prejudice the soil toward roses and strawberries."

—Samuel Coleridge's Diary, (07-27-1830).

~

Martin Luther said there is no greater comfort on earth than baptism. He wrote: "Bapitazitus sum. I am baptized, and God—who cannot lie—has made an eternal covenant with me." Throughout Luther's tumultuous life, when overwhelmed by depression, problems, doubts, or sin, he would exclaim, "Bapitazitus sum. I am baptized." He was remembering who he was. His personal feelings at any particular moment were not the issue. At issue was his baptism, wherein God's eternal love was shown to him. Eternal love was not dependent on Luther's faithfulness but on the faithfulness of God.

~

During a California senatorial contest several years ago, one of the candidates was maligned badly. A voter wired him:

> *A report receiving wide circulation here that your children have not been baptized. Telegraph denial immediately.*

The reply came back:
> *Sorry to say, report is correct. I have no children.*

—Jacob Braude

~

CHRISTIAN

A Christian should be an Alleluia from head to foot!
—*Augustine.*

~

A Christian is one who believes that the Bible is God's inspired word, wondrously suited to the spiritual needs of one's neighbors. —*Anonymous.*

~

Promise me that if you become a Christian you'll become a Presbyterian.
—*Lord Beaverbrook to Josef Stalin in 1941.*

~

A man fell into a pit and couldn't get himself out. Several people came by and made their comments:

> A sympathetic person: *I feel for you down there.*
> An objective person: *It's logical that someone would fall down there.*
> A self-righteous snob: *Only bad people fall into a pit.*
> A Calvinist: *Endure the pit to the glory of God.*
> A self-pitying person: *You haven't seen anything until you've seen my pit.*
> An optimist: *Things could be worse.*
> A Pessimist: *Things will get worse.*

A Christian took him by the hand and lifted him out of the pit, and said, " I'll take care of you until you recover."

~

Look up the word Christian in your dictionary and you will find some bizarre definitions. For example, Webster says, "A Christian is a decent, civilized, and presentable person." I can envision a dedicated Scottish Christian reading this and having to brace himself with a Scotch and soda. Such tripe caused Martin Luther to lament that the Church, "...was producing declawed, defanged pussycats, instead of Christ's tigers."

~

A driver did the right thing, stopping at the crosswalk even though he could have beaten the red light by accelerating through the intersection. The tailgating woman behind him went ballistic, pounding on her horn and screaming in frustration because she missed her chance to drive through the intersection with him. Still in mid-rant, she heard a tap on her window and looked up into the face of an intense police officer. The officer ordered her out of her car with her hands up. He took her to the police station where she was searched, finger-printed, photographed, and placed in a cell. After a couple of hours, another policeman approached the cell and opened the door. She was escorted back to the booking desk where the arresting officer was waiting with her personal effects. He said, "I'm awfully sorry for this mistake. You see, I pulled up behind your car while you were blowing your horn, flipping the guy off in front of you, and cussing a blue streak at him. I noticed the 'Choose Life' license plate holder, the 'What Would Jesus Do' bumper sticker, the 'Follow Me to Sunday School' bumper sticker, and the chrome plated Christian fish emblem on the trunk. Naturally—I assumed you stole the car."

~

There are only three kinds of Christians:
> *Rowboat Christians, who have to be pushed wherever they go;*
> *Sailboat Christians, who move with the prevailing wind;*
> *Steamboat Christians, who know where they should be going and go.*

~

Most of my friends are not Christians. But I have some friends who are Anglican and Roman Catholics. —*Dame Rose Macaulay, (1881-1958)*

~

When the Emperor Constantine turned Christian, he banned the eating of sausage, which of course, immediately created a whole army of sausage bootleggers and may explain why Al Capone always looked like a sausage.
—*Donald E. Westlake*

~

We decree and order that from now on, and for all time, Christians shall not eat or drink with Jews, nor admit them to feasts, nor cohabit with them, nor bathe with them. Christians shall not allow Jews to hold civil honors over Christians, or to exercise public offices in the State. —*Pope Eugenius IV, (1421-1447).*

~

A Christian is a man who feels repentance on Sunday for what he did on Saturday and is going to do again on Monday. –*Thomas Ybarra.*
Christians have burned each other, quite persuaded that all the Apostles would have done as they did. –*Lord Byron, English poet. (1788-1824).*

~

If a man cannot be a Christian in the place where he is, he cannot be a Christian anywhere. —*Henry Ward Beecher.*

~

> *I fear that Christians who stand*
> *With only one leg upon earth,*
> *Also stand with only*
> *One leg in heaven.*

Dietrich Bonhoeffer, Letter to his fiancee,(08-12-1943).

~

COMMITMENT

At the end of the Sunday School Hour, three students told their parents that their teacher said they were crazy. The parents were irate and confronted the teacher. "We heard you told our children we were crazy." The teacher disagreed..."Oh, no! I didn't say anything like that. I said that you ought to be committed."

~

A London newspaper reported on a trustee of the British Vegetarian Society and member of its national council who resigned his position after he was discovered selling hamburgers at a store in his village.

~

Whatever. — *Bumper sticker.*

~

Commitment is healthiest when it is not without doubt, but in spite of doubt.
— *Rollo May, Psychologist.*

~

The dilemma of the United States was summarized in a headline in the Tallahassee Democrat on July 28, 1984. It read: "Polls: We're Religious, But Not Committed."

~

The minister gave a sermon on *total giving*. When the offering plate came to his pew, one small boy looked up at the Usher and asked, "Could you lower the plate?" Thinking that he wanted to see into the plate, the Usher held it down a bit. "No," said the boy, "a little lower, please." The Usher lowered the plate even further. "More—could you just put it on the floor?" The boy stepped into the plate and stood there, and said, "This is what I give to the Lord."
—*William Phillippe, A Stewardship Scrapbook.*

~

A young man in college was determined to do anything to improve his grades. He bought a large comfortable chair that invited serious study. He bought warm slippers and a loose fitting jacket. A book stand that would hold his book at exactly the right angle was placed beside the chair. He bought a special reading lamp. After supper, he'd take off his coat, put on the study jacket and slippers, adjust the lamp, place his book on the stand at the right angle, get into a comfortable position—and fall asleep. — *Unknown.*

~

Just think of it. One-seventh of your life is lived on Mondays.

~

Be decisive—more or less. — *Poster.*

A pious old gentleman stood up and prayed:

Use me, O Lord--
In some advisory capacity.

~

In the winter of 1994, an Alabama church raised $2,500 by staging a *Coon Hunt for Christ.* — *"Harpers' Bazaar", (08-1995).*

~

O Thou Great Chief, light a candle in my heart—that I may see what is herein—and sweep the rubbish away from Thy dwelling place. — *"An African Schoolgirl's Prayer".*

~

Theodore Roosevelt said of Taft:
He means well, feebly.

~

At an Ordination Exam, a clerical examiner was determining if a seminarian was dedicated to God and His Kingdom. "Yes! I am," the candidate confirmed. The examiner probed deeper, asking if that meant he was willing to even be damned for the glory of God. The candidate pondered his reply. "No, sir—I don't believe I am; but—I'm perfectly willing for *you* to be damned for the glory of God."

~

All alone in the North woods and walking towards his cabin a mile away, a man saw a black bear stalking him. All he had was his knife. The bear kept getting closer and closer, and the man started to pray. "Lord—if it is Your will to have me kill this bear—let me do it with one plunge of the knife, so I'm not mauled in the process. But—Lord—if it is Your will that I be killed by this bear, let him do it with one swipe of his paw—so I don't meet a slow and painful death. But, oh God—if you are neutral—You are about to see the best bear fight You ever saw!"

~

If a man does not keep pace with his companions,
Perhaps it is because he hears a different drummer.
Let him step to the music he hears,
However measured or far away.
> —*Henry David Thoreau.*

~

The chicken approached the pig, asking if he would like to make a contribution for the ham and egg breakfast at the church. "You don't have to give a whole lot, but you should give something." The pig replied, "That's easy enough for you to say. For you it's a donation; for me, it's total commitment!"

~

COMMUNITY

The Talmud tells of several men who were in a boat. Suddenly one took out a drill and began to make a hole beneath his seat. When the others protested, he inquired, "What does it matter to you? You complain, but I'm only boring this hole under my own seat

~

After the game, the King and the pawn return to the same box. —*Italian proverb.*

~

I'm told that on the crowded trains and train platforms in India there are two distinct communities—those on the train and those trying to get on the train. There is a fierce allegiance in each community. Whenever a crowded train pulls into a station, the people on the platform struggle and maneuver and push to get on. The passengers already inside the train, on the other hand, are pushing back because the train is already crowded. Nevertheless, once one is on the train, one belongs to a different community and turns around to try and keep the others off.

~

A big rainstorm and flood in Tennessee threatened the crops and livestock. A farmer looked out his window the next morning to discover that the neighbor farmer had driven over in his horse-drawn wagon. The neighbor said, "Fred, I hate to tell you, but last night that storm washed all your hogs away and—they're all drowned." Fred frowned and asked, "Well—how about your hogs?" The neighbor said, "Mine are all drowned too." Fred inquired, "How about Covington's hogs?" His neighbor said, "Covington's hogs are all drowned, too." Fred put his hands on his hips and said, "Well—it's not as bad as I first thought." That is more than misery loving company. It is also about finding strength and consolation as one faces adversity *with* one's neighbors.

~

We are learning that in a crisis, we don't just save ourselves, we save each other.
—*Julia Roberts, addressing victims of 9-11.*

~

Let him who cannot be alone beware of community … Let him who is not in community beware of being alone. —*Dietrich Bonheoffer.*

~

Describing the Great Wall of China is like explaining the Grand Canyon. One has to see it to believe it. It is massive and cost an immense amount of money and human lives to build. It seems impregnable, but three times the enemies of China breached it. Not by breaking it down, or going around it, or climbing over it. They did it by bribing the gatekeepers.

~

I slipped up behind one of my members one afternoon in the grocery store and put my hands over her eyes. She said, "Who is it?" An observer answered for me. "It's a man, a handsome man." I liked her immediately. After my friend recognized my voice we had a brief conversation. Next Sunday, she said, "Jim, I want to thank you for what you did for me the other day." I did not know what she meant, as I'd forgotten our chance meeting. She went on, "You know—when you put your hands over my eyes in the store. When I was a young girl, my Mother and Father were very affectionate, and so was my husband. But now that I'm a widow and live alone, nobody touches me anymore. It was good to be touched."

~

After Lefty Gomez wound up his career in the major leagues, he became manager of the Yankee Farm Team in Binghamton, New York. But, his best managerial achievements were in keeping his tremendous sense of humor. One day a rookie runner was on second and another man on first. The batter hit a line drive to right field, and both runners took off at top speed. The rookie started for home then paused—to make sure that Gomez, coaching third, had waved him home. He glanced back at Gomez, wavered when he saw the throw coming in, and then slid back into third—just in time to meet the runner from first zooming in with a great slide. Gomez looked at both of his runners sprawled over third base. "Oh, what the heck," he laughed, and slid in to join them. —*Herman Masin, Curve Ball Laughs.*

~

There's a rule in sailing that the more maneuverable ship should give way to the less maneuverable one. I think that's a good rule for human relationships too.
—*Dr. Joyce Brothers.*

~

The power secret of the church: *Anything I can do, WE can do better.*

~

Tell me—I'll forget. Show me—I may remember. Involve me—and I'll understand.
—*Chinese proverb.*

~

We may have come over on different ships, but we're in the same boat now.
—*Whitney Young.*

~

We who are strong ought to bear the infirmities of the weak.
(Romans: 15:1, RSV)

These are powerful, life-giving spiritual words. The critical word, of course, is we. If the word were they, it would be just another lament from the defeated lambs passing a resolution against the wolves. But Paul's word, we, presupposes strength. It presupposes right relationships with one another. It presupposes righteousness, which alone exalts a nation. It is the haves of the United States who are to bear the infirmities of the weak. Wouldn't it be the most beautiful sight in the world to see the strong—financially strong--ilitarily strong--intellectually strong--connectedly strong--spiritually strong--gather voluntarily in a great convocation in every city to consider how we might do with a little bit less, so that those who have the least can survive with dignity? —*Ernest Campbell*

~

CONFESSION

If you think you have no sin—that makes one more.

~

The prosecuting attorney described the defendant's crime as the work of a master criminal, and carried on in a most skillful and clever manner. The defendant rose and said, "Sir flattery will get you nowhere. I won't confess."

~

You needn't spend much time in the South before you will hear one of the older folk say, *Lawdy Mercy!* Now, *Lawdy Mercy* has several meanings. It could mean surprise and happiness over good fortune. In times of sadness or despair, you will often hear someone say *Lawdy Mercy*. I don't even know how to spell *Lawdy Mercy*. But there must be some connection to the traditional words of confession in the Christian Church, *Kyrie Eleison*, that we say. It means, *Lord have mercy*. Sometimes in worship we repeat the words, *Kyrie Eleison*, with the same casualness with which southern people use the term *Lawdy Mercy*. We don't really come to grips with what we are saying because we haven't come to grips with the depth and agony of our sin, or how desperately we need the Lord's mercy.—*Roxana Atwood*

~

Frederick the Great once visited a prison and talked with the inmates. Each one said they were falsely accused and imprisoned. Finally the King stopped at the cell door of a man who said nothing. "Well," said the King, "I suppose you're innocent too?" The prisoner answered, "No Sir. I'm guilty. My punishment is just." The King told the Warden, "Set this scoundrel free before he misleads all these fine innocent people in here."

In her baseball book, *Wait Till Next Year*, Doris Kearns Goodwin, a staunch Brooklyn Dodger fan, tells of her first confession. She confessed to the priest that she had wished harm on other people. She began her litany: "I wanted Allie Reynolds to break his arm." The priest asked, "You mean the Yankee Pitcher? And how often did you make this wish?" She answered, "Every night in my prayers." And were there others?" he inquired. "Oh, Yes. I wished Robin Roberts of the Phillies would fall down the steps and that Richie Ashburn would break his hand. I wished Enos Slaughter of the Cardinals would break his ankle, and that Alvin Dark of the Giants would hurt his knee. But, I wished all these injuries would go away once the baseball season ended."

~

One of the most authentic confessions I've heard came from a little boy, Dean Maskell. His letter enclosed a rubber communion cup holder. "Dear Reverend Atwood, I found this wine holder in my toy box. I didn't mean to steal it. I just took it out of curiosity. I have put it in the package. I really am sorry. Dean Maskell."

~

Mea Culpa, Mea Culpa! Lord, we're sorry. We don't know exactly why we did it, but we did it and we're sorry. We'll try not to do it again. But, being human, we probably will. We'll be sorry then too.

~

Pooh Bear persuaded Piglet to join him in an expedition to capture a heffalump. They made their way to a sycamore tree in the middle of the forest. Pooh Bear spied what he thought were heffalump tracks and followed them around the tree. Once, twice, three times. As they started on their fourth time around the tree, Christopher Robin, who saw the whole chase from his perch on the limb, called down to Pooh, "Silly old Bear. What are you doing?" Pooh Bear stopped and scratched his head. He put his foot in one of the tracks and said, "I see now. I have been foolish and deluded, and I am a bear of no brain at all." But Christopher Robin, hearing his friend's confession, threw his arms around Pooh and said, "You're the best bear in all the world!" —*A.A. Milne, Winnie the Pooh.*

~

The Catholic Priest spent four hours hearing confession in a nunnery. When he exited from the confessional booth, he was exhausted and told his colleagues, "Hearing confessions from the nuns is like being stoned to death with popcorn."

~

The Rabbi of Lelov said to his Hasidim, "A man cannot be redeemed until he recognizes the flaws in his soul and tries to mend them. A nation cannot be redeemed until it recognizes the flaws in its soul and tries to mend them. Whoever permits no recognition of his flaws, be it man or nation, permits no redemption. We can be redeemed to the extent to which we recognize ourselves. Then Jacob's sons said to Joseph: 'We are upright men,' he answered, 'That is why I spoke to you saying: ye are spies.' But later, when they confessed the truth with their lips and hearts, and said to one another, 'We are verily guilty concerning our brother,' the first gleam of their redemption dawned. Overcome with compassion, Joseph turned aside and wept." —*Hasidic tale.*

~

The elder priest, speaking to the younger priest, said, "I know you were reaching out to the young people when you had bucket seats put in to replace the first four pews. It worked. We got the front of the church filled first. The young priest nodded and the old one continued, "And, you told me a little more beat to the music would bring young people back to church, so I supported you when you brought in that rock and roll gospel choir that packed us in all the way to the balcony." The young priest asked, "So—what's the problem?" The elder priest said, "I'm afraid you've gone too far with the drive-thru confessional." The young priest protested. "My confessions, Father, have nearly doubled since I began that!" The priest agreed and continued, "However, my son, the flashing *Toot'n Tell or Go to Hell* neon sign really has to go."

~

Four clergymen went fishing together. The Anglican priest suggested they deepen their casual friendship to one of mutual trust and support. "We've never really shared our real needs and problems. I need to confess to you. I have a fondness for alcohol and must watch myself carefully, or I could become an alcoholic." The Roman Catholic Priest was moved by his friend's honesty. "I, too, have a problem," he said. "Often, I yearn for female company. I'd love to take a beautiful woman out to eat and talk over a nice dinner; but, I can't risk it." The Methodist preacher said, "Confession is good for the soul. As you know, our church is small—and so is my salary. I confess that I took twenty dollars out of the collection plate so I could buy my son a new pair of shoes." The fourth preacher listened—but kept looking at his watch. "I must go—NOW." The others protested, "You owe us some honesty. We've been painfully honest with each other, confessed our problems and sins." He agreed. "Gentlemen—my sin is gossip. I can't help myself, and--I can't wait to get back to town."

~

At a revival meeting, a man got up and rambled on and on about what a miserable wretch he had been. I've done every conceivable bad thing one could do. I've been a contemptible swine, but I never knew it until now." A weary fellow on the front row said, "Oh, sit down. The rest of us knew it all along.
--*Charles W. Byrd.*

~

Now I've laid me down to die, I pray my neighbors not to pry
Too deep into the sins that I, not only cannot here deny,
But much enjoyed as life flew by
--*Preston Sturges, American film director.*

~

CONVERSION
(NEW CREATION)

Up to 30,000 years ago man could boast a proud evolutionary record, but since then no physical improvement has occurred in the human species.

--Earnest Hooton, American anthropologist.

~

Even in slight things the experience of the new is rarely without some stirrings of foreboding. —*Eric Hoffer, "The Ordeal of Change".*

~

So sing Alleluia whether you do it like Sills or Pavarotti or croak it like a crow. In or out of tune, it will make sweet music today. Let the sounds flow into your ears and the truth stream into your hearts. And do not be afraid to cry. If you are a new creature in Christ you will be happy in your tears. —*Gerard Sloyan.*

~

If we are to perceive all the implications of the new, we must risk, at least temporarily, ambiguity and disorder. —*Gordon, "Creative Computing".*

~

One thing new is the prevalence of newness; the changing scale and scope of change itself, so that the world alters as we walk in it.

— *J. Robert Oppenheimer, Dynamics of Change", (1967).*

~

"What's it like to be married to a professional football player?" one wife was asked. She said, "It's really exciting to be married to a line-backer. Every time he comes home he looks like a different person. One time he has fewer teeth, another time, more stitches, another time he limps up the walk. I don't know what he'll look like after the next game." —*"Presbyterian Outlook."*

~

I know a grandmother who was sick in body and spirit when her daughter-in-law died. All she could do was to grieve about her daughter-in-law's death and worry about her son and grandchildren. What were they going to do? She got a call from her son, who asked her to live with him and help him take care of the children. When she first arrived, she was so frail she could hardly climb the stairs. But soon—strength came back to her legs. And power came back to her body, and energy returned to her spirit. She had discovered she was needed. Her son needed her; her grandchildren needed her. There are thousands of people who need you. Are you connected to one or two?

~

A man in Kansas City went to the stockyards and bought an old horse. Then, he called a moving company and made arrangements for them to deliver it to his seventh floor apartment. The horse couldn't fit into the elevator so it was led up seven flights of stairs. The moving company employee took it into the man's room. "Here's your horse, Mister. That will be thirty-five dollars, please." The gentleman replied, "No, you're not through yet. Here's a gun. Take it into the bathroom, shoot it, and put it in the bath tub." The fellow did as instructed. Then he said, "Mister, I've been working for this company for twenty-seven years, and I've met some strange people and done some 'way-out things', but this beats all. Do you mind telling me what this is all about?" The husband said, "Sure. My wife and I both work. I get home about thirty minutes before she does every day. So every single day she comes bounding into the house asking, 'What's New? What's New? What's New?' Today I'm going to tell her, 'There's a dead horse in the bathtub.'"

~

When the bathtub was introduced in Cincinnati, the newspapers predicted rheumatism and inflammation of the lungs. Some cities banned its use. Musicians groaned and laughed at Richard Wagner's compositions. Westinghouse scientists were called fools because they were trying to stop a train with air brakes. Stan Musial was told a person could never hit the way he stood in the batter's box. Being skeptical before that which is brand new can be costly.

~

Billy Graham was once on a crowded airliner flying to Charlotte, North Carolina. On the same flight right in front of the evangelist was a man who was drunk and was filling the air with profanity. One gentleman took things in hand and asked the man if he knew that Billy Graham was sitting behind him. At that the bleary-eyed fellow struggled to his feet and said, "Billy Graham? Put 'er there," extending his hand. "I'm really proud to meet you. Your sermons sure have helped me a lot, and I want to thank you."

~

Charles Peaker, a Canadian, vouches for this epitaph:

> *Here lies Miss Arabella Bim*
> *She was so very pure within*
> *She broke the outer shell of sin*
> *And hatched herself a cherubim.*
> —*James H. Weekley, Church Chuckles.*

~

In Tolstoy's book, *My Religion*, he says, "Five years ago I came to believe in Christ's teachings, and my life suddenly became changed: I ceased desiring what I had wished before. What formerly appeared good to me appeared bad, and what had seemed bad appeared good. . . The direction of my life, my desires became different: what was good and bad changed places."

~

A man complained bitterly to his minister that he had not had a dramatic conversion experience. "Why hasn't God knocked me off some horse like he did the Apostle Paul?" She reminded him when the Almighty goes hunting for sparrows, God doesn't use cannonballs.

Mort Walker, in his comic strip, "Beetle Bailey," has a great segment: The General is in deep thought. "I can't understand it. We split the atom. We conquer space. We cure disease. We make all kinds of fantastic inventions. But we can't seem to do a thing with PEOPLE."

~

A good friend who was a Catholic Priest told of a colleague who had an exceptionally bad day at work. He decided to take off his clerical collar and go see a movie and forget his bad day. The movie was not good. On his way home someone met him on the street and inquired, "Mister, are you born again?" He replied, "You're damn right I am!"

~

I have known men who thought the object of conversion was to clean them as a garment is cleaned, and that when they were converted they were to be hung up in the Lord's wardrobe, the door of which was to be shut so that no dust could get at them. A coat that is not used the moths eat; and a Christian who is hung up so that he will not be tempted—the moths eat him; and they have poor food at that.

—Henry Ward Beecher.

~

Sir Winfred Grenfeld, the famous missionary doctor in Greenland, while in medical school in Chicago saw a big tent where Dwight L. Moody was conducting an evangelistic mission. He stepped inside to see what was going on. He writes: "It was very new to me … and then a tedious prayer bore began with a long, long portion." When Dwight L. Moody had enough of the man's prayer, he stood up and in a loud voice said, "Let us sing a hymn while our brother here finishes his prayer." Moody's practical side interested Grenfeld and he stayed the entire service. When he left, it was with the determination to live as a Christian.

~

Michael Weisser, the cantor at a Lincoln, Nebraska synagogue, found himself the target of the local Grand Dragon of the Ku Klux Clan, Larry Trapp. Trapp was constantly calling Weisser and harassing him, trying to drive him out of town. When the late night calls and hate mail came he knew where it was coming from and he was afraid. But, he called his tormentor back only to get his answering machine. After listening to the prerecorded anti-Semitic message, he calmly offered to take Trapp, who was an invalid, out to the grocery store. For weeks he kept at it, leaving recorded messages to help the Grand Dragon. Finally, Trapp called back and complained, "What do you want? You're harassing me." Soon, Trapp called back saying, "I want to get out of this, but I don't know how." Weisser responded, "I'll bring dinner and we'll talk." His wife brought along a silver ring as a peace offering. When they met face to face, the Klansman and the Cantor, Larry Trapp burst into tears. Trapp eventually moved in with the Weissers, who cared for him as his health declined. In time, he converted to Judaism. –Source Unknown.

~

Martin Luther said there are three conversions: the conversion of the heart; the conversion of the mind; and the conversion of the purse.

A woman in her early forties has a heart attack and is taken to the emergency room in the hospital. While there she has a near-death experience and asks God, if this is when she is to die. God explains to her that she has another forty years to live. When she is dismissed by her physician she decides to stay and have a facelift, liposuction, breast augmentation, a tummy tuck and other cosmetic surgery. A beautician comes and changes her hair color and style. When she walks out of the hospital she is hit by an ambulance and killed. When she arrives in heaven she asks God, "I thought you said I had another forty years?" God replies, "I didn't recognize you."

~

Clovis Chappel compared different types of conversion experiences to training horses on his Tennessee farm. There were two ways to break wild horses. One way was to put a horse in a corral and then walk around him for a few days until he grew accustomed to humans. Then they would flip a rope over his neck; the next day they would put a blanket on him and then in a few days, a saddle. In another few days, they would pull it tight. Then they would walk around him, leaning on him all the while. Finally, they would jump on and ride. The other way was to have a bronco buster who would mount the wild horse and ride him until he was exhausted. In a day or two the horse would be broken. If you asked the horses when they were "converted," the one ridden by the bronco buster could tell you the day and the hour. The other might even answer as Socrates did: "Search me."

~

A player on the Philadelphia Phillies described a teammate: "We turned his life around. He used to be depressed and miserable, now he's miserable and depressed."

~

He had gone forward at the evangelist's invitation for the last four years. This time he prayed fervently, "Oh, Lord, fill me. Fill me with your Holy Spirit." But an elderly member kneeling at the rail replied, "Don't do it, Lord. He leaks. He leaks."

~

Mary Lyon, 19th century educator, was a teacher of Emily Dickinson. One day she invited those who "wanted religion" to meet with her in Room B. Emily Dickinson left her books to slip into the crowded classroom. The evening's session took the form of a series of questions:

> *Did the gathered impenitents feel they were willing to give up the world?*
> *Were they ready to bow their will to God, to see their portion in Him?*

After readings from the Bible and prayers, Lyon asked all those who wanted this day to be entirely employed in the service of Christ to stand. Emily felt she could not in good conscience rise. The girls around her stood, one by one, until all in the room were on their feet except Emily. There she sat, small and rigid, and solemn-eyed, looking straight ahead. It was a very conspicuous thing for her to do. She was far from unconcerned with her religious condition, yet she appeared the opposite to those in that hushed room. In later times Emily explained the matter quite simply to a friend.

> *They thought it queer I didn't rise.*
> *I thought a lie would be queerer.*

It was a small incident, misunderstood, but, as is frequently the way, it was whispered around the school, from student to student and teacher to teacher. From that time on all kept an eye upon her progress in becoming a Christian.

--Polly Longsworth, Emily Dickinson: Her Letter to the World.

~

Time makes more converts than reason. —*Thomas Paine, Philosopher.*

~

If a man approaches you with the obvious intent of doing you good, you should run for your life. —*Henry David Thoreau.*

~

George Sawyer in his book, *Jack, C.S. Lewis and His Times*, tells of the conversion of the great Christian author. The conversion took place on Sept.22, 1931, while Jack was sitting in the sidecar of Warren's motorcycle en route to Whipsnade, the safari zoo. "When we set out, I did not believe that Jesus Christ was the Son of God," Jack wrote, "and when we reached the zoo I did." It was not an emotional conversion, nor was he aware of his reasoning. "It was more like when a man, after a long sleep, still lying motionless in bed, becomes aware that he is now awake." Maybe the motorcycle ride scared him into the Kingdom.

~

George Burns tells of his first success as an entertainer: "When I was 7 years old, I was singing with three other Jewish kids from the neighborhood. We called ourselves the Pee Wee Quartet. A local department store held a talent contest representing all the local churches. When the Presbyterians had no one to enter, the minister asked the four of us to represent them. There we were, four Jewish boys, sponsored by a Presbyterian Church and our opening song was *When Irish Eyes are Smiling*. We followed with *Mother Machree* and won first prize. The Church got a purple velvet altar cloth and each of us kids got an Ingersoll watch worth about 85 cents. I was so excited I ran all the way home to tell my mother. She was on the roof hanging out wash. I hollered out, 'Mama I don't want to be a Jew any more.' She calmly said, 'Do you mind my asking why?' Well—I said—I've been a Jew for seven years and never got anything. I was a Presbyterian for 15 minutes today and I already got a watch.' My mother answered, 'First--help me hang up the wash. Then you can be a Presbyterian.'" —*Unknown.*

~

If I were a cassowary on the plains of Timbuktu, I would eat a missionary, Cassock, band, and hymn-book too. --*Samuel Wilberforce, Abolitionist.*

~

CROSS
(SACRIFICE)

The Rabbi and the Priest sat together at the boxing match. One boxer at the beginning of the first round made the sign of the cross. The Rabbi turned to the Priest and asked, "Does that do him any good?" The priest replied, "Not if he can't box."

~

A woman said to the clerk at a jewelry store, "I'm interested in a cross." Opening the display case, she paused. "Do you want a plain one or one with the little man on it?"

~

A grizzled old trapper came out of a Texas swamp to hear for the first time the story of the crucifixion. The preacher ended the sermon lamenting its tragedy. The old trapper, ignorant of the Scriptures, but steeped in the traditions of Texas, rose up and said, "All I can say is, it was just too bad the Texas Rangers weren't there."—*Ross Phares, Bible in Pocket, Gun in Hand.*

~

St. Vincent de Paul once made a person, who would not go to Communion, promise that each night for a week he would agree to kneel before the cross and kiss it three times, repeating with each kiss, "I don't care, I don't care. I don't care."

~

A little boy named Bron went to church for the first time with his governess. He liked the singing but was distressed to learn a terrible piece of news. It was about a brave and kind man who was nailed to a cross. Still later, he began to weep because nobody else seemed very upset. Bron's lips were trembling. His governess looked at him and said, "Bron, don't take it to heart, son. Don't take it to heart. Somebody will think you are strange."—*From a novel by C.E. Montague.*

~

Why sacrifice now so that you can be wealthy when you're dead?

~

After a terrible forest fire in Yellowstone Park, a National Park Ranger found a bird literally petrified in the ashes, perched like a statue on the ground at the base of a tree. When he knocked over this eerie sight with a stick, three tiny chicks scurried from under the dead mother's wing. The mother bird could have flown to safety but refused to abandon her little ones.

Actually, there are only two philosophies of life: one is first the feast and then the headache; the other is: first the fast and then the feast. Deferred joys purchased by sacrifice are always the sweetest.—*Fulton J. Sheen.*

~

Truth is always in danger of being sacrificed on the altars of good taste and social stability. — *William Sloane Coffin.*

~

The contemporary church is so often a weak, ineffective voice with an uncertain sound. It is so often the arch-supporter of the status quo. Far from being disturbed by the presence of the church, the power structure of the average community is consoled by the church's silent and vocal sanction of things as they are. But the judgment of God is upon the church as never before. If the church of today does not recapture the sacrificial spirit of the early church, it will lose its authentic ring, forfeit the loyalty of millions, and be dismissed as an irrelevant social club with no meaning for the 20th century.

— *Martin Luther King, Jr., Letters From A Birmingham Jail.*

~

The most difficult sermon to preach and practice is self-denial.—*Ethan White.*

~

The mice which helplessly find themselves between the cat's teeth acquire no merit from their enforced sacrifice. –*Mahatma Ghandi.*

~

Good manners are made up of petty sacrifices.—*Ralph Waldo Emerson*

~

One half of knowing what you want is knowing what you must give up before you get it.—*Sidney Howard.*

~

The problem with Paul's "*living sacrifice*" is it keeps crawling off the altar.

--*Stephen Gaukroge..*

~

In the United Nations building in New York there is a stained glass mural of the history of humankind which depicts the bloodshed, terror, and tragic loss of life which has been the scourge of war. In the background, women and children are crying and cities and homes devastated. At the focal point, there is a cross which seems to beckon the nations to peace. What is interesting about that mural is that the artist, Chagall, claimed to be an atheist. But his message is one Christians should know. Namely, there is no hope, peace, or reconciliation; there is no future for us or our children apart from a love which is willing to be broken so that nations will not learn war anymore.

~

In the 1940's and 50's, French Archaeologist, Paul Thoby, traveled throughout Europe to churches claiming to have a piece of the actual cross on which Jesus died. He did an iconographic and archaeological examination of these ancient relics brought back by the crusaders. Having studied each particular piece, he was forced to conclude that the cross was at least 50' high, 25' wide and 10' thick, and was made of 50 kinds of wood. --*Cross and Crucifix: Its History and Origin (French).*

~

It is curious that people who are filled with horrified indignation whenever a cat kills a sparrow can hear the story of the killing of God (in Christ) told Sunday after Sunday and not experience any shock at all. —*Dorothy Sayers.*

~

A friend, Ray Epperson, taught English language to immigrant children in the Arlington County (VA) School System. He was seated at a reading table when one of the children came up behind him and began to feel the back of his neck. Ray wondered what was happening. Then the little boy said, "No chain on your neck. No chain for a cross. You must be very poor if you don't have a cross."

~

When an opposing batter crossed himself before stepping into the batter's box, Yogi Berra said to him, "Oh, why don't we just let the Lord watch the ball game?"

~

Righteousness on the cross is more powerful than triumphant evil on the throne.
—*Martin Luther King, Jr.*

~

I simply argue that the cross be raised again at the center of the market place as well as on the steeple of a church. Jesus was not crucified in a cathedral between two candles, but on a cross between two thieves; on the town garbage-heap; at a crossroads so cosmopolitan that they had to write his title in Hebrew, Latin, and Greek, at a place where cynics talk smut, and thieves curse, and soldiers gamble. That is where He died. And that is what He died about. And that is where church men and women should be and what churchmanship is all about."
—*Sir George Macleod, Only One Way Left.*

~

Rev. Ewing sent me a nice letter because God laid my address on his heart (along with 20,000 others). It is a very generous invitation to receive his Prosperity Cross which will give me the, "Power to Get Wealth." This is no ordinary cross, and quite unlike the cross upon which Jesus suffered. The Prosperity Cross is of beautiful golden metal and has been blessed with prayer for my spiritual, physical and financial blessings, and it's free. Ewing advised me to take the Lord as my partner, reminded me I had nothing to lose, and urged me to let God help me. He quoted several Biblical texts, all of which were superimposed over pictures of split-level homes, jet planes, cars, computers, TVs, washers and dryers, and lots of money." But—I lost his address—and I'm still poor.

~

There is nothing scandalous about the pretty crosses suspended in our sanctuaries or the silver crosses we wear around our necks. But, if we searched for some contemporary symbol which carries the sort of offensiveness which the cross imparted to first century men and women, it might be the electric chair. Instead of a smooth, shiny cross with no splinters, perhaps, the sign of a dark, dirty electric chair will serve to startle our complacency about the means used to get rid of the prophet from Nazareth. —*Milton S. Carothers.*

~

The way of the cross is the way of everlasting life. He that will take up that burden and carry it willingly will yet find it to be such a burden as wings are to a bird and sails are to a ship. —*Samuel Rutherford.*

~

After World War II, a play came out of Germany, written by Gunter Rutenborn, and called, *The Sign of Jonah.* In that drama God is on trial for creating an unjust world in which suffering is not in proportion to our sinfulness. The prosecution witnesses included men, women, and children who did not deserve the torment they had experienced. At the conclusion of the trial the jury brings in the verdict. God is found guilty as charged. The judge pronounces the sentence. God is condemned to earth to suffer the same fate as his creatures.

~

No blessing's trail can be traced far back without running upon blood—that at the end of every road, down which a benediction comes, there stands a cross.
-- *Harry Emerson Fosdick, sermon fragment.*

~

A particular congregation had a big church fight. In the sanctuary there was a bare wall broken only by two tablets in memory of two former pastors. Some of the members wanted to replace those tablets with a cross; others thought that was blasphemy. The church split, one group formed a new church called, "The Church of the Cross."

~

The cross is the clenched fist of humanity victoriously shoved into the face of God. It is the shriek of pain, the sob of distress, the cry of anguish from those who will have none of God. —*Leo Rippy, Jr.*

~

Somewhere in literature is the story of a village green which was bought as the site for a shortwave radio station. The workmen were to come in and remove a stone cross which had stood there for centuries. It was large and deep set and a difficult task. The village idiot observed the struggle of the workmen and sat down and began to sing in a childish chant:

> *They can't pull the cross over;*
> *They can't dig up the cross;*
> *The cross is from the beginning;*
> *It's too deep;*
> *It's at the core of creation.*

~

DEATH

Epitath Dustin Hoffman wants on his grave.

~

Dr. Elizabeth Kubler Ross, the Swiss psychiatrist, who has helped us in the western world deal more realistically with death, wrote; "If I were expecting a baby, I would call my other children and say let's think of some names for the baby. What might we like to call the baby? If we knew it would be a boy, perhaps we might paint his bedroom blue. If it were a girl, we might paint the bedroom pink; and if we didn't know and didn't care, we'd paint the room yellow. But we would talk about it. It would be the most normal thing in the world." She concludes, "If we talked about our own death in the same way, our lives would be lived quite differently."

~

"If somebody has a bad heart, they can plug this jack in at night as they go to bed and it will monitor their heart throughout the night. And the next morning when they wake up dead, there'll be a record." —*Mark Fowler, FCC Chairman.*

~

Whoever has lived long enough to find out what life is knows how deep a debt of gratitude we owe to Adam, the first great benefactor of our race. He brought death into the world. –*Mark Twain.*

~

Death is the great equalizer, not because it makes us equal, but because it mocks our pretensions at being anything else. In the face of death, differences of race, class, nationality, sexual orientation all become known for the trivial things they ultimately are. —*William Sloane Coffin.*

Stranger, call this not a place of fear and gloom. To me it is a pleasant spot, it is my husband's tomb. —*North Dakota epitaph.*

~

This body sleeps in dust
Immortal joys await the host
In perfect beauty may it rise
When Gabriel's trumpet shakes the skies
—*Long Island, NY epitaph.*

~

When H.G. Wells was dying, he said to those around his bedside, "Don't bother me. Can't you see I'm busy dying?" And on another occasion he said, "Go away. I'm all right."

~

Ron Culberson, of The Northern Virginia Hospice, developed a fine relationship with a middle aged woman who was an outpatient. When her condition worsened, she was moved to the inpatient care unit. On her arrival he visited her. "Nancy, it's so good to see you. We're glad you're here." She replied, "Thanks, Ron, I've just been dying to see this place." As soon as the words were out, both of them threw back their heads and laughed. That was followed by a tender exchange and God's time for healing.

~

In John Gunther's little book, *Death Be Not Proud,* he writes of his courageous son, John Jr. who was terminally ill with cancer. His output of urine had to be carefully measured each day. To add some spice to this daily, boring event, John Jr. went to great pains to purchase some goldfish. He put them in a fresh catheter bag beside his bed and placed the regular catheter bag on the other side. He waited to see the Doctor's face when he made his rounds. Indeed--death be not proud!

~

My work is done. Why wait? —*George Eastman, of Eastman Kodak, in his suicide note.*

~

Turn up the lights. I don't want to go home in the dark.—*O. Henry, last words.*

~

A Chinese emperor once asked a wise man to take a month and figure out the meaning of happiness. When he returned, the wise man said, "Happiness is when the grandfather dies, then the father, and then the son."

~

He passed on. She passed away, fell asleep, made her exit, gave up the ghost, was gathered to her ancestors. He has gone to glory (a brave assumption). He went west, she bit the dust. He kicked the bucket. She hopped the twig. He was called home. She croaked. We will say almost any fool thing to avoid using the words, 'dying,' or 'died' or 'dead'." —*Anglican Digest.*

James Michener, in his book, *Rascals In Paradise*, tells of a gentleman in the 1930's who had a suspicion that a great war was on the horizon. After he consulted with some military experts, he bought some property on the only secure refuge from the world's insanity. It was a little place called, Guadalcanal.

~

The Angel Gabriel appeared to a great golfer and said, "I have good news and bad news. The good news is that there is golf in heaven. The bad news is your tee time is 8:00 a.m. tomorrow."

~

A man moved to a small town to avoid rush hours and the congestion of the city. The first week he was run over and killed by the Welcome Wagon.

~

When the Surgeon General's first report came out linking cancer and smoking, people wondered how fundamentalists in the Bible Belt would connect this new knowledge with tobacco's influence in the local economy. Jack Spong, later to become Episcopal Bishop of Newark, was then a rector in the South. He reported that folks down there were taking it pretty cool. "Hell," they say. "Anybody can quit smoking. Takes a <u>man</u> to face cancer!"—"*Context*".

~

Obituary: DIED: Salvador Sanchez, 23, World Boxing Council Featherweight Champion and one of the sport's best fighters; of injuries after his Porsche 928 collided with two trucks, just north of Queretaro, Mexico. A school dropout at 16, Sanchez once said, " I found out that I liked hitting people, and I didn't like school, so I started boxing." A peppery tactician, he wore opponents down for late round knockouts. His record: 43-1-1. "I'd like to step down undefeated," he said last month. "I'm only 23 and I have all the time in the world."

~

We accept death for others but not for ourselves. Recall the holiday cartoon of the pig and turkey that passed on the road and exchanged season's greetings. Next frame shows the pig imagining the turkey ready for carving. The turkey, on the other hand, saw the pig with an apple in his mouth on the holiday table.

~

I know a lot of people who died at 30 and were buried at 65.

~

A 92 year old man managed to save $3,000 dollars and asked his broker for some financial advice. The broker suggested his buying a three-year CD. The old gentleman was startled. "Son, at my age, I don't even buy *green bananas*."

~

The academicians were gathered at the Faculty Lounge to pay tribute to their colleague. Said one to another, "Poor old Smith. He published and published, but he perished anyway."

~

The best way to get praise is to die. —*Italian proverb.*

"Your food stamps will be stopped effective March 1, because we received notice that you passed away. May God bless you. You may reapply if there is a change in your circumstances. —*Department of Social Services, Greenville, S.C.*

~

I look upon life as a gift from God. I did nothing to earn it. Now—that the time is coming to give it back—I have no right to complain.--*Joyce Cary.*

~

Dear Don Gustavo, we have to take things as they are. I've had a long life and served the church and left some mark on history. By God's grace I haven't behaved badly: so, not a day more. If the Lord wants me to remain a little longer, well and good, otherwise—we're off. —*Pope John 23rd, in a letter to his friend.*

~

Ed White, Executive of National Capital Presbytery, relates a friend's experience in ministering to the dying. His friend learned that a childhood friend was dying of cancer in their home town. What he didn't know was that her family hadn't yet told her. They were afraid *she wouldn't be able to handle it.* He walked into her hospital room and said, "Hello, Bella, I hear that you are dying." Bella responded, "Thank God—at last there's someone I can talk to." She knew what was going on. It was her family that couldn't handle it, and as a result, they were of little help to Bella.

~

Death—a distant rumor for the young. —*Andy Rooney.*

~

Paul Elmen was saying good-bye to his colleague, Anglican-Catholic theologian Julian V. Langmead Casserly. "Only days before he died, a bright neurologist came into his room to test his neural reflexes. He held up three fingers. 'How many fingers do I have?' he asked. No response from Julian. 'Now, how many fingers do I have?' holding up four fingers. Again, silence from Julian. The doctor left the room, shaking his head at this failure of response. When he had gone Julian beckoned his friend, the Rev. Charles Moore, who was sitting at the bedside. 'Any good neurologist has five fingers,' he whispered."— *"Context"*

~

The Church History Professor was dying. Family and friends gathered at his bedside. One thought he had already died. "Feel his feet. No one ever died with warm feet." The learned professor opened one eye and said, "Joan of Arc did."

~

"Am I dying or is this my birthday?"
        —*Nancy Astor, on seeing her children gathered around her bedside during her final illness, (1964)*

~

An old gentleman was getting a physical before marrying a young woman. The doctor asked admiringly, "How old are you, Sir? The old gentleman replied, "Eighty-seven." The doctor asked, "And the bride?" The old fellow said, "She's twenty- three." The doctor predicted, "That kind of disparity in your ages could be fatal." The old gentleman shrugged, "If she dies, she dies."

~

A woman, seriously ill, met the Pastor who tried to comfort her about her future. He said, "Louise, you don't need to worry or fret about a thing. Soon you will be going to your home." She looked up and said, "I know that. But I don't know which home."

~

So this is death! Well! —*Ludwig Von Beethoven, (1827).*

~

One's final words and actions often reflect the life one has lived. For example, the final words of the French grammarian, Dominique Bouhours were, "I am about to—or I am going to die. Either expression is correct." And Dr. Joseph Henry Green, an anatomist, monitored his own vital signs right up until the very end. Taking his own pulse, he looked up and said to his physician, " Stopped!" It was. He fell back dead at that instant.

--*James Thorson, A Funny Thing Happened On the Way to the Morgue.*

~

Three days after death, hair and fingernails continue to grow but phone calls taper off. —*Johnny Carson.*

~

If you live to be a hundred you have it made because very few people die past the age of a hundred. —*George Burns.*

~

The Texas rancher incurred the wrath of his family when he requested that he be buried in his four-wheel drive pick up truck. His wife said, "What in the world are you thinking about?" He calmly replied, "I've never been in a hole it couldn't get me out of."

~

Graveyards are full of indispensable people. —*Charles de Gaulle.*

~

A woman with a serious illness asked her doctor how much time she had left. He replied, "Mrs. Smith, I believe you have about six months to a year. But you could get a second opinion." She went from this doctor's office on the third floor to see a doctor on the first floor, and asked him the same question. "Doctor, how much time do you think I have left?" Being a very religious man he responded, "Mrs. Smith, whatever the Man Upstairs says you have left will be the time you have." She replied, "I just spoke with the man upstairs and he said I have from six months to a year." —*Mary Bell.*

~

Death: When your subscriptions to "Time" and "This Week" run out.

Good-bye, proud world! I'm going home; Thou art not my friend; I am not thine.
—Ralph Waldo Emerson.

~

Erma Bombeck's epitaph request: "Big deal, I'm used to dust."

~

Death: catching up with our baptism.

~

In a cemetery in Indiana is this epitaph:
Pause stranger when you pass me by,
As you are now, so once was I.
As I am now, so you will be,
So prepare for death and follow me.
Someone passed by and read those words and scratched this reply:
To follow you I'm not content
Until I know which way you went.
—James S. Hewett.

~

My Dad's last words: "I never felt better in my life. I think I'll take a nap."
—H.D. Atwood.

~

I'm always amused when I hear someone say, "**IF** *I should die."*

~

When the mighty oak is felled the whole forest echoes with its fall, but a hundred acorns are sown in silence by an unnoticed breeze. *—Thomas Carlyle.*

~

The statistics on death are quite impressive. One out of one people die.
—George Bernard Shaw.

~

The tragedy of life is not in the fact of death, but in what dies inside of you while you live. *—Norman Cousins.*

~

I know I'm going to die, but I don't want to be there when it happens.*—Yogi Berra.*

~

Martin Luther King, Jr. wrote "If a man happens to be thirty-six years old, as I happen to be, and some great truth stands before the door of his life, some great opportunity to stand up for that which is right, and just, and he refuses to stand up because he wants to live a little longer, or he's afraid his home will be bombed, or afraid he'll lose his job, or afraid he'll get shot—he can go on and live till he's eighty, but the cessation of breathing in his life is merely the belated announcement of an earlier death of the spirit. A man dies when he refuses to stand up for that which is right; a man dies when he refuses to take a stand for that which is true."*—Letters from a Birmingham Jail.*

~

DISCIPLES

If the Lord wanted us to go metric, He'd have chosen 10 disciples.

~

A soldier once asked one of Buddha's disciples to describe the master's teaching: *Do good—avoid evil—and keep your mind pure.* The soldier protested, even a five year old child knows that! The disciple replied: *Maybe so—but few men—even at 80—can practice it.*

~

The bumper sticker warned that the automobile would be suddenly "unmanned" if the rapture came. At a stoplight the driver behind pulled alongside and inquired, "If the rapture comes, can I have your car?"

~

In case of Rapture, this T-Shirt will be minus one great bod. —T-shirt.

~

Many of us want to serve God—but only as advisers. —*Anonymous.*

~

The General confronted a soldier: "Craig, consider this: Your company is pinned down by fierce machine gun fire from the top of the hill. Your commanding officer asks, 'Do we have any volunteers?' What would you do, Craig?" Craig replied, "I'd immediately hunker down in the trench, Sir, so as not to get in the way of any of the volunteers."

~

President Abraham Lincoln regularly attended worship at The New York Avenue Presbyterian Church when he was president. One evening, walking home to the White House, an aide asked the president what he thought of Doctor Gurley's sermon. The president replied in fragmented phrases: *...content excellent...eloquent...forgot the most important element...forgot to ask us to do something great!*

~

A Park Ranger at a campfire in Idaho was comparing walking toward the sun and walking away from it. He revealed that when you walk toward the sun, there is no darkness, no shadow; but when you walk away from the sun, your shadow is always in your way. That is true of the s-u-n, and it is also true of those following the S-o-n of God.

~

A new Pastor confided to his mentor: "Where the Apostle Paul went, there were riots. But—where I go—they serve me tea.

~

The most difficult sermon to preach and the hardest to practice is self-denial.
—*Ellen White.1991).*

James Atwood

Leave a Message
(A country-gospel song, sung to any generic country tune.)

Yesterday I got a call from Heaven, and I answered on the second ring,
But it musta been a bad connection, 'cause I couldn't hear a doggone thing!
Well, my office was full of distractions, and I guess my equipment's old,
And-- I really didn't mean to do it—but I kinda put the Lord on hold. So...
Chorus:
Leave a message for me, Jesus; start talkin' at the sound of the beep,
'Cause I might be busy on my other line, or I just might be asleep.
But I've had a rotten day at the office, and I just can't go it alone,
So--if I don't answer when you call me, Lord—leave a message on my
Code-a- phone!

Well, I'm sorry that I cut you off, Lord, and I really meant to call you back—
Would have left to myself (a memo on my message board)
But—I couldn't find a tack.
Oh--it's a high-speed, high-tech world now Lord—
I know you understand What I mean.
So--if you want to reach a busy person like me Lord—leave a message on The
phone machine...OH—Please...(repeat chorus*) —Mary Cox, (11-06-1991)

~

Miguel de Unamuno was a Spaniard who lived in exile and was considered to be a heretic. He was, however, a great Christian, patriot, writer, and evangelical leader. When he was yet a young man he wrote the epitaph he wanted placed on his grave. He knew he would be following his Lord, and that the barometer of his life would always register *stormy*. The epitaph he composed read:

Lay me in thine eternal bosom Father—For from life's fierce struggle, I come—
All undone.

~

When Sri Lanka was taken over by a communist regime, few attended worship, and the leadership tried to symbolically bury the church. They declared Sunday a workday and Monday a weekly holiday. Yet, people got up at 5:00 a.m. on Sunday to worship before going to work and attendance grew. It was a disaster for the government, so Sunday was changed back to a holiday. Subsequently, worship attendance dropped to its previous level.

Church history bears witness that tough standards or requirements do not turn people away from following Jesus. To the contrary, sacrifice and dedication continue to claim men and women who would follow Jesus.

~

Lamented Martin Luther to fellow clergy: "The church is producing declawed, defanged pussycats instead of Christ's tigers."

~

He who marries the spirit of the age will surely be a widower in the next.
—G. K. Chesterton.

~

30

DISCIPLINE*

"EXCUSE ME, I HAVE TO WORK ON MY
SERMON ON FASTING."

~

When the stomach is full, it's easy to speak of fasting.

—*Jerome, 4th C.*

~

A street musician was playing near 42nd Street in New York City when a professional violinist asked, 'How can I get to Carnegie Hall?' He responded, "Practice, man, practice!" —*Anonymous.*

~

Actually there are only two philosophies of life: one is first the feast and then the headache; the other is first the fast and then the feast. Deferred joys purchased by sacrifice are always the sweetest. —*Fulton J. Sheen.*

~

An old Irish ditty says: "To live above with the saints we love, ah, that is the purest glory; to live below with the Saints we know, ah, that's another story."

--*John Powell, A Reason To Live! A Reason to Die.*

~

A mother told the nanny looking after her child that she didn't want to hear him cry for any reason. Whatever he wanted, he was to have. Soon after the conversation, the child was wailing, and the mother rushed to the back of the house. "What's all of this racket?" she inquired. The nanny asked if she had meant it when she said the child was to have whatever he wanted? "Absolutely," said the mother. "That's what I thought—so I let him catch the bee he was chasing."

~

When my son was in high school, I'd say, "Son, it's time to get up and go to school. Are you up?" He'd answer, "Yeah, I'm up." Ten minutes would pass by, and I'd ask him, once more, if he was up. Again, he would answer, "Yeah, I'm up." In five minutes, not seeing any signs of activity, I'd go to the door and find him fast asleep. Being awakened and getting up are not the same.

~

People are unreasonable, illogical and self-centered.
Love them anyway!
If you do good, people will accuse you of selfish, ulterior motives.
Do good anyway!
If you are successful, you will win false friends and true enemies.
Succeed anyway!
The good you do today will be forgotten tomorrow.
Do good anyway!
Honesty and frankness make you vulnerable.
Be honest and frank anyway!
The biggest folks with the biggest ideas can be shot down by
the smallest folks with the smallest minds.
Think big anyway!
People favor underdogs but follow only top dogs.
Fight for some underdogs anyway!
What you spend years building may be destroyed overnight.
Build anyway!
People really need help but may attack you if you help them.
Help people anyway!
Give the world the best you have and you'll get kicked in the teeth.
Give the world the best you've got anyway!
—Bishop Muzorewa.

~

Without discipline there is no life at all. —Katherine Hepburn.

~

What we do on some great occasion will probably depend on what we already are; and what we are will be the result of previous years of self-disciplined. —H.P. Liddon.

~

You will never be the person you can be if pressure, tension, and discipline are taken out of your life. —James Bilkey.

~

*That straight and narrow path we hear so much about always
receives the most wear right around the edges.*

~

It's ominous for the future of a child when the discipline he receives is based on the emotional needs of the disciplinarian rather than the child's needs.
Gordon Allport, *Personality and Social Encounter.*

~

* See, also, Perserverance.

32

DREAM
(VISION)

If I have seen further, it is by standing on the shoulders of giants.
—Sir Isaac Newton.

~

The first white man at The Grand Canyon wrote in his diary, "Today we came across a large desolate gully. Obviously, nothing good will ever happen, here."

~

Religion has to mean more to us than a commitment to ethical behavior, to loving our neighbors. It has to teach our eyes how to see the world.
—Rabbi Harold Kushner, Who Needs God?

~

The obscure we see eventually; the completely apparent takes longer.
—Edward R. Morrow, Journalist.

~

The further backward you can look, the further forward you're likely to see.
—Winston Churchill.

~

One man said to an artist, "I never see any sunsets like you paint." The man replied, "No, Sir. Don't you wish you could?"

~

Yes, I'm a dreamer. For a dreamer is one who can only find his way by moonlight, and his punishment is that he sees the dawn before the rest of the world.
—Oscar Wilde.

~

I wear my wife's eyeglasses because she wants me to see things her way.
—Jason Feinburg.

~

The prospects never looked brighter and the problems never looked tougher. Anyone who isn't stirred by both of these statements is too tired to be of much use to us in the days ahead. *—John W. Gardner.*

~

He who is narrow of vision cannot be big of heart. *—Chinese proverb.*

~

Worse than being blind would be to be able to see but not have any vision.
—Helen Keller.

~

On a dog sled only the lead dogs' view changes.

A cynic is one who sees things as they are and not what they ought to be.
—*Ambrose Bierce.*

~

Only eyes washed by tears can see clearly. –*Louis Mann*

~

You see things and you say, "Why";
But—I dream things that never were and say, "Why not?"
--*George Bernard Shaw*

~

In the country of the blind,
The one-eyed man is king.
--*Erasmus*

~

Vision: the art of seeing things invisible.—*Jonathan Swift.*

~

Be a Columbus to whole new continents and worlds within you,
Opening new channels, not of trade—but of thought.
—*Henry David Thoreau, Walden.*

~

It's kind of fun to do the impossible. —*Walt Disney*

~

Personals Ad in the Atlanta Journal:

SINGLE BLACK FEMALE seeks male companionship, ethnicity unimportant. I'm a very good looking girl who LOVES to play. I love long walks in the woods, riding in your pickup truck, hunting, camping and fishing trips, cozy winter nights lying by the fire. Candlelight dinners will have me eating out of your hand. Rub me the right way and watch me respond. I'll be at the front door when you get home from work, wearing only what nature gave me. Kiss me and I'm yours. Call (404) 875-6420 and ask for Daisy.

Over 15,000 men found themselves talking to the
Atlanta Humane Society about an 8-week-old black Labrador retriever.

~

In an article in the "*Christian Science Monitor*" (09-19-1991), a teacher is quoted as saying a real poet "…has the strength to keep others' dreams—even after they're lost for years. Or—mislaid."

~

Dream of the person you would like to be—waste the person you are. —*Unknown.*

~

You know you are old when you give up your dreams for memories. —*Anonymous.*

Napoleon met briefly with Robert Fulton, the inventor of the steam engine. He asked the inventor, "Are you telling me you can make a ship sail against the wind and currents by lighting a fire under her decks? I have no time to listen to such nonsense."

~

A boy was born 'mid little things, between a little world and sky,
And dreamed not of the cosmic rings, round which the circling planets fly.
He lived in little works and thought where little ventures grow and plod,
And paced and plowed his little plots, and prayed unto his little God.
But as the mighty system grew, his faith grew faint with many scars,
The cosmos widened in his view, but God was lost among the stars.

Another boy in lowly days, as he to little things was born,
But, gathered lore in woodland ways, and from the glory of the morn.
As wider skies broke on his view, God greatened in his growing mind;
Each year he dreamed his God anew, and left his older God behind.
He saw the boundless scheme dilate, in star and blossom, sky and clod;
And as the universe grew great, he dreamed for it a greater God.
—*Sam Walter Foss (1858-1911).*

~

To make your dreams come true you have to stay awake.
—*Bob Phillips.*

~

Any man with ambition, integrity, and $10,000,000 can start a daily newspaper.
–*Henry Morgan.*

~

Richard Haliburton's dream as a youth was one day to spit a mile.

~

It's no use waiting for your ship to come in unless you've sent one out.
—*Belgian proverb.*

~

After he won the lottery a man was asked what he would do with his money. He replied, "I'm going to buy me a double-wide and move to Alabama."

~

The world is made of dreamers and doers.
What we need most of all are dreamers who do.
—*Eleanor Roosevelt.*

~

Two soldiers were talking about religion. One described what the dream expressed in the Gospel meant to him. The other ridiculed the Christian story as a colossal pipe dream. The dreamer replied, "Well, I can't think of a dream I'd rather have come true than that one."

~

ETERNAL LIFE

A five year old boy in the North Phoenix Baptist Church quoted John 3:16 "For God so loved the world that he gave his only begotten Son that whoever believe in Him shall not perish but have everlaughing life! —*More Holy Humor.*

~

God put me on earth to accomplish a certain number of things. Right now, I am so far behind, I will never die. —*Anonymous*

~

It's kind of fun to do the impossible. —*Walt Disney*

~

The way of the cross is the way of everlasting life. He that will take up that burden and carry it willingly will, yet, find it to be such a burden as wings are to a bird and sails are to a ship. —*Samuel Rutherford.*

~

Cricket is a game the English (not being a spiritual people) have invented in order to give themselves some conception of eternity. —*Lord Mancroft.*

~

Although she was often invited, an elderly woman never had time to go to church. One of her neighbors told her, "Mrs. Jones, at your age, you ought to be thinking more about the 'hereafter.'" She replied, "Honey, that's all I do. I go from one room to the other and ask myself, "What am I here after?"

~

I preach Christ to you, not because you may die tomorrow, but because you can live today. —*George Whitfield.*

~

Question: *If you could live forever, would you and why?*

Answer: *I would not live forever, because we should not live forever. Because if we were supposed to live forever, then we would live forever, but we cannot live forever, which is why I would not live forever.* —*Miss Alabama, Miss USA Contest (1994).*

~

The poet, Robert Frost was great friends with his neighbor, Rabbi Victor Reichert. Just a few months before his death, when Frost was 88 years old, he said to Reichert, "Victor, what do you think are the chances of life after death?" Reichert, threw the discussion back to Frost. "Robert, what do you think?" He bent his head and was silent for a long time. Then lifting his face toward Reichert, he said …. "With so many ladders going up everywhere, there must be something for them to lean against." —*Victor Reichert, The Rabbi and the Poet.*

Mark Twain has a delightful story on "Captain Stormlove's Visit to Heaven." When he arrives, he opens the door to a huge room overflowing with used harps. He asks St. Peter about the used harps and St. Peter replies, "When folk arrive here no one wants a used harp. Everybody wants a new one when they come to heaven. They plan on sitting on some cloud and playing it for eternity. But we've discovered they strum it a day or two and then get tired of that. They bring the harps back and go looking for something more exciting to do."

~

I went to the woods because I wished to live deliberately to front only the essential facts of life, and see if I could not learn from what it had to teach, and not when I came to die, discover that I had not lived.
— *Henry David Thoreau, Walden.*

~

In Tennessee Williams' play, *Suddenly Last Summer*, Mrs. Venable visited the doctor. Their conversation:

Doctor: *What was it about this that fascinated your son?*

Mrs. Venable: *My son was looking for —, she stopped with a slight gasp, and continued, let's just say he was interested in sea-turtles.*

Doctor: *That isn't what you started to say.*

Mrs. Venable: *I stopped myself just in time.*

Doctor: *Say what you started to say.*

Mrs. Venable: *I started to say that my son was looking for God and I stopped myself—because I thought you'd think—"Oh, a pretentious young Crackpot."*

~

As a youth, I remember hearing eternity defined *as living on a rock which is a hundred yards long and a hundred yards wide*. Every ten thousand years a sparrow comes to that rock and sharpens his beak. When the rock is ground to dust—that is just the beginning of eternity. That meant something to me as a youth—when I believed **that big is always better** and I was more impressed with **quantity than quality**. But quantity and the length of eternity is not my concern today.

~

FAITH

"I'm not unmindful of man's seeming need for some kind of faith. Basically, I'm for anything that gets you through the night. Be it prayer, tranquilizers, or a bottle of Jack Daniels." —*Frank Sinatra.*

~

Carl Jung was once asked, "Do you believe in God?" Jung responded, "I don't believe in God. I know God."

~

In 1970, the World's Fair was in Osaka, Japan, and many Christian institutions and missionary homes were deluged with young people from the United States who came "to witness to their faith" and, of course, catch the Fair. They had very little money in their pockets and needed a free place to stay and an occasional meal. Some of us asked about their welfare. They answered, "God will provide." But, one missionary who lived closest to Expo wasn't so sure. Her analysis was: "They call it *God*? I call it mooching."

~

This morning," said the minister, "I'm going to speak on the relationship between fact and faith. It is a fact that you are sitting here in the sanctuary. It is also a fact that I am standing here speaking. But it is faith that makes me believe that you might be listening to what I have to say. –*Anonymous.*

~

"It's good for us to open our minds to wonder and awe and, without science, we're helpless children. But without a deep religious faith to accompany our scientific knowledge, we become blundering fools, reeling about in our new and terrible cock-sureness—into one disaster after another." —*J.P.Priestly, novelist.*

~

The great act of faith is when man decides he is not God.
--*Oliver Wendell Holmes, in a letter to William James, (1907).*

~

Listen to the psychiatrist, Carl Jung, who spent his life helping his patients make sense of theirs. "During the past 30 years, people from all the civilized countries of the earth have consulted me. I've treated many hundreds of patients, but among all my patients in the second half of life, that is to say, those who are over 35, there has not been one whose problem in the last resort was not that of finding a religious outlook on life. It is safe to say that everyone of them fell ill because he had lost that which the living religions of every age have given to their followers, and none of them has been really healed who did not regain his religious outlook on life."

~

When the news of the invention of the telephone was reported to Professor Tait of Edinburgh, he said, "It's all humbug. Such a discovery is physically impossible." When the Abbe Moigno first showed Edison's phonograph to the Paris Academy of Science, all those present declared: "It is impossible to reproduce the human voice by means of a metal disc." Abbe was accused of hiding a ventriloquist under the table. —*William Barret, Irrational Man.*

~

We can understand the plight of the famous Dr. John Jowett of Oxford who, so runs the tradition, inserted "used to" in a muffled voice, when he recited the creed: *I used to believe in God the Father Almighty.*

~

He had a kind of faith, in that the church he did not attend was Methodist.

~

A renowned agnostic astronomer sat next to an equally famous theologian on a coast to coast flight. After some conversation the astronomer turned to the theologian and said, "I've done a bit of reading in the Bible and theology, and I've concluded that your field can be boiled down to "Jesus loves me this I know for the Bible tells me so." The theologian rubbed his chin for a moment and replied, "Yes, there's much truth in what you say. I've also done some reading in your field of astronomy and I've concluded that all astronomy can be summed up in "Twinkle, twinkle little star."

~

Nothing like blind belief so fosters its opposite.— *William Sloane Coffin.*

~

The pastor of a Baltimore Presbyterian church was the main speaker at a conference in Montreat, North Carolina. Early one morning there was a knock at his door.

      Pastor: Uh, yes, yes. What is it? Who is it?
      Voice: Doctor--it's John. It's time for early morning prayer meeting.
      Pastor: Early morning prayer meeting? ...what time is it?
      Voice: Five o'clock.
      Pastor: Five o'clock!! I don't even believe in God at 5 o'clock in the morning!

~

Anne Young, a visiting nurse who had great faith and was a strong believer in prayer, ran out of gas on her way home. Considering the resources at her disposal she took several urinals she had stored in her trunk, went to the gas station, made her way back to her car, and began pouring gas from the urinals into her tank. A tough old geezer pulled alongside and said, "Lady, I don't think it will work, but I wish I had your faith."

~

Faith is believing what you know ain't so.—*Mark Twain.*

~

In Robert Bellah's book, *Habits of the Heart,* he tells of a young nurse, Sheila Larson, who describes her faith as *Sheilaism.* She says, "I believe in God. I'm not a religious fanatic. I can't remember the last time I went to church. My faith has carried me a long way. It's *Sheilaism*—just my own little voice."

~

The Mother was 95 years old and knew that death was near. She was of Old New England stock and wasn't very demonstrative or emotional about her faith. Her daughter, on the other hand, was demonstrative and emotional and wanted to provide every comfort for her beloved Mother. She'd spend hours at her bedside speaking of God's faithful promises. "God is with you, Mother—God loves you, Mother—we are all saved by the grace of God—Christ has prepared a glorious place in heaven for us and will take us to Himself." Her Mother was tired and needed rest, so she opened one eye and said, "Yes, Ginny, I've seen that program."—*Personal conversation with Ginny Thornburg.*

~

That which enters the mind through reason can be corrected: That which is admitted through faith, hardly ever. —*Santiago Ramony Rajal.*

~

I'll stick to Christ as a burr to an overcoat.
—*Last words, Katherine von Bora, wife of Martin Luther.*

~

A minister's son seemed to get dirtier than most kids. One evening, he came to the table dirtier than usual. His father said, "Junior, go wash your hands. They've got germs on them." Heading for the bathroom, the son muttered, "Germs! Germs! Germs and Jesus! Germs and Jesus! That's all I hear around this house and I've never seen either one of them!"

~

Seven-eights of everything can't be seen.
—*Unknown.*

~

There is a time when one must stand up for what one believes…I believe I'll have another piece of pie.—*Anonymous.*

~

The obscure we see eventually, the completely apparent takes a little longer.
--*Edward R. Murrow.*

~

The things fisherman know about trout aren't facts. They are articles of faith.
—*John Gierach, Trout Bum (1986).*

~

Some people use their faith like they do a bus.
They are ready to ride if it is going their way.

~

FORGIVENESS

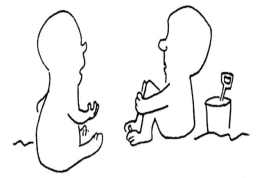

" BEFORE YOU CAN BE FORGIVEN, YOU HAVE TO SIN! "

~

The Scotsman, Martin Elginrod left instructions for this epitaph on his tombstone:

Here lie I, Martin Elginrod.
Have mercy on my soul, Lord God.
As I would do were I Lord God,
And ye were Martin Elginrod.

~

I love that street sign: *U-Turns permitted.*

~

It's easier to get forgiveness than permission.

~

The Day of Atonement atones for offenses of man against God, but it does not atone for offenses against man's neighbor, till he reconciles his neighbor.

—*Jewish Mishnah.*

~

Remember the famous line in Eric Segal's Love Story? "Love is never having to say you're sorry." The corollary is: "Love is never having to forgive."

~

The afternoon preceding his assassination, President Lincoln issued a pardon for a soldier sentenced to death for desertion. Signing it he said, "I just think the boy can do more good above the ground than under the ground."

~

I do not know the reason why, but whenever I clean my garage, I feel thoroughly cleaned of all my sins and a feeling of joy comes over me.

Reading of the struggles to end apartheid, I was moved by an article about Nyameka Goniwe, the widow of a black activist, who was killed in 1985 by the South African Government. The Government said at that time that her husband should be "…permanently removed from society as a matter of urgency." High Government Officials were put on trial for his death. Mrs. Goniwe, who works in Capetown for the Church, said that she would settle for an official admission that the Apartheid State used its machinery to kill its opponents. Said she, "What could heal me inside is for this Government to own-up and say, 'Yes, we did it.' In exchange for that, I'd be willing to forgive and to try for a national reconciliation. I regard that as a challenge. I challenge myself to forgive."

~

Letter from a student to the Dean at John Abbot College in Montreal: "I am hereby returning my identification card since I had deliberately lied about my date of birth. I was helped to discover this by the police. If it would be possible, I would like to get a new I.D. card." *— "Chronicle of Higher Education".*

~

A city revolted against its ruler. The King set forth to subdue and punish it, and the city hastily requested a pardon. At a distance from the city, the elders came and begged forgiveness. "For your sake," the King said, "I forgive one-half the guilt." At the gates of the city the masses turned out and pleaded for mercy. "For your sake," said the King, "I forgive half the guilt that is left." When he entered the city and found all the little children gathered with song and dance and joy to appear before him, he exclaimed: "For your sake, I forgive everything!" and the King joined in their celebration. *—Jewish midrash.*

~

Rabbi Harold Kushner in his book, *When Bad Things Happen to Good People,* asks an ultimate question: "Are we capable of forgiving and loving the people around us, even if they have hurt us and let us down by not being perfect? Can we forgive them and love them because there aren't any perfect people around and because the penalty for not being able to love other imperfect people is condemning ourselves to loneliness?"

~

We pardon in the degree that we love. *—Francois de la Rochefoucauld.*

~

One of the shameful chapters of this country was how many of the comfortable, especially those who profited from the misery of others, abused her. But she got even in a way that was almost cruel. She forgave them.
—Ralph McGill, speaking of Eleanor Roosevelt.

~

Often after two folks have an argument, one can't seem to forgive and the other can't seem to forget. The Gospel says God does both.

~

FUNERAL

NBC reported the death of a movie actress in Hollywood whose last wish was to be buried in a lace nightgown, sitting in her favorite Ferrari. Her family protested and the funeral was postponed until the judge granted her wish.

~

O mighty Caesar! Doth thou lie so low?
Are all thy conquests, glories, triumphs, spoils,
Shrunk to this little measure?
—*Shakespeare, "Julius Caesar",*
Act 3: the words of Antony.

~

A Chinese valet asked his employer for permission to attend the funeral of a close friend. "That will be fine," said the employer. "And I suppose you'll put some food on the grave as you Chinese usually do?" Mr. Wong admitted that this was so. "Look here, Wong, when do you think your friend's going to eat that food?" Mr. Wong replied, "He'll eat the food at the same time your friends wake up and smell your flowers."

~

Daddy was walking his little girl through the cemetery, examining various tombstones, when all of a sudden she shouted, "Daddy, come quick. This one isn't dead." Hurrying over he read the epitaph that intrigued his daughter, "He is not dead, but sleepeth."

~

Tombstones usually provide one's date of birth and date of death, with a dash in between. By the way--what are you doing with your dash?

~

As usual the Super Bowl was a sell out. One fan was surprised to see an empty seat in front of him. He expressed how unusual it was to a woman seated nearby. She explained it belonged to her husband who recently died. "I'm very sorry," responded the man. "Really, I'm surprised another relative or friend wouldn't jump at the chance to take his seat." She looked up with equal surprise on her face. "Me too," she said. "They all went to the funeral."

~

It makes me sad to realize I'm going to miss my funeral by just a few days.
—*Garrison Keillor.*

~

A little boy described his experience at a burial service. "...then—the minister went to the casket and said a prayer *...In the name of the Father, and the Son and in the hole he goes.*"

~

All men are cremated equal.

A young preacher was asked by the local funeral director to hold a grave-side burial service at a small local cemetery for someone with no family or friends. The preacher started early but quickly got himself lost, making several wrong turns. Eventually, a half-hour late, he saw a back hoe and its crew, but the hearse was nowhere in sight, and the workmen were eating lunch. The diligent young pastor went to the open grave and found what appeared to be the vault lid already in place. Taking out his book, he read the service. Feeling guilty because of his tardiness, he preached an impassioned and lengthy service, sending the deceased to the great beyond in style. As he was returning to his car, he overheard one of the workmen say: "I've been putting in septic tanks for twenty years and I ain't never seen nuthin' like that." —*Anonymous.*

~

Intriguing name in Niagara Falls, NY: ***Amigone Funeral Home.***

~

No one's death should go unnoticed. However, there was not much news about Larry La Prise, who died in early February, 2005. He was the man who wrote "The Hokey Pokey," to which many of us danced. He died peacefully at age 93. The most traumatic part for his family was getting him into the coffin. They put his left leg in and then the trouble started.

~

Here lies Johnny Yeast.
Pardon me for not rising.
— *Epitaph in Ruidoso, New Mexico.*

~

Haine Haint. --*Epitaph of Arthur Haine of Vancouver, Washington.*

~

At the funeral home, the minister took several minutes to praise all the good qualities of the deceased. One worshiper asked his friend, "Do you suppose they sent us to the right room?"

~

Persons in the U.S. spend $1 billion a year on gravestones so they can be remembered.

~

The funeral industry in America reports today's trend is toward personalizing one's casket. We personalize everything else, why not our own death? One designer makes "Art Caskets," featuring images such as Our Lady of Guadalupe, cherubs, and Aids awareness ribbons. A golf enthusiast ordered his own Fairway to Heaven. Those with an irreverent sense of humor can choose a coffin that appears to be a brown paper parcel stamped with red letters, "Return to Sender." For space agers and $5,000, a few ounces of remains can be placed aboard commercial satellites and sent into low earth orbit. In 2001, a deep space mission was planned to blast remains out of the solar system.—*"USA Today", (03-17-1999).*

~

GRACE

Charles Spurgeon told of a minister colleague who went to the home of a poor woman in his congregation with an offer to pay her rent. He knocked again and again but there was no response. The old woman was there all the while but didn't open the door. Later she explained, "I heard the knocking but I thought it was the man who had come to ask for the rent."

~

A large friend of mine, Leon Howell—along with his slim wife—visited a finely appointed Chinese home. They were invited to sit in antique chairs. Her chair shattered—his didn't. Leon calls that grace.

~

Grace means that God grades on the curve, and if the curve is set by Jesus, then maybe all of us pass. —*Anonymous.*

~

A Presbyterian elder died and went to heaven. Saint Peter asked why he should be allowed in. The elder replied, "I've been an elder in the Presbyterian Church for thirty-four years and I never missed a session meeting. I was our Church's official representative to Presbytery and once I was elected to be a Commissioner to The General Assembly." St. Peter was impressed and said, "That's wonderful! My friend, it takes 100 points to get in here and that will give you one point. Anything else?" The elder looked a bit worried. "Well, I have 58 years of perfect attendance in Sunday School. I have badges to prove it. I taught an Adult Sunday School Class for nineteen years." St. Peter said, "Really? I can't believe it!" When assured it was the truth, the Great Apostle said, "That will be worth one point." The elder really began to get worried. He quickly added, "I always ran my business according to the golden rule. I was always fair to my employees; their raises were always higher than the cost of living increase. I believed in EEO before it was law in our country." Again St. Peter said, "That's tremendous! That also is worth one point!" Exhausted, the Elder sighed, "Well—I can see—if I get into heaven it will only be by the grace of God!" And Peter said, "Why, that's worth 99 points!"

~

"May the Great A-Priori intellectual integrity of the eternally regenerative Universe, grant glorious flight to the new born."
—*Benediction, Unitarian Church, Kennebunkport, Maine; quoted in "Context".*

~

When my son was five years old he ran his first competitive race and finished next to last in the fifty yard dash. With tears in his eyes he sobbed, "Daddy, do you still love me?"

~

You and I can—and do—mess up, but we can't finally blow it—because God is great and God is good. —*Anonymous*

Mercy imitates God and disappoints Satan. —*St. John Chrysostom.*

~

Get place and wealth, if possible, with grace; if not—by any means, get wealth and place.—*Alexander Pope.*

~

We serve shrimps, crabs, tall people—and a lot of nice people, too.
—*Sign in an Alexandria, VA fish market.*

~

Bruce Larson tells of a Catholic Priest in the Philippines who was a much loved man of God, but carried a secret burden in his heart about a sin he committed when in seminary. He had confessed it to a priest when it happened, but he still had no peace and no sense of God's forgiveness. Now, there was a woman in this priest's parish that deeply loved God and claimed to have visions in which she spoke with Christ. The priest was skeptical of her claims and wanted to test her. He said:

> *You say you actually speak directly with Christ in your visions? Let me ask you a favor. Next time you have one of these visions I want you to ask Jesus what sin your priest committed when he was in seminary.*

The woman agreed and went home. When she returned to the church a few days later, the priest asked her if Christ had visited her dreams, and she said He had. The Priest then asked the woman if she had remembered to ask Jesus what sin her priest had committed when he was in seminary:

> **Yes, I asked Him—Jesus said He didn't remember.**

~

John Newton thought himself to be an unlikely candidate to meet God. Usually, one does not think of the Captain of a slave ship—with all that vocation denotes—as a likely candidate to meet our Savior. But when we sing *Amazing Grace*, we are singing the hymn Newton wrote about his meeting with God.

> *Amazing grace, how sweet the sound, that saved a wretch like me.*
> *I once was lost, but now I'm found; was blind but now I see.*

~

> **And all the wickedness in this world**
> **That man might work or think**
> **Is no more to the mercy of God**
> **Than a live coal in the sea.**
> —*William Langland, (14th C).*

~

Flannery O'Conner often said, "Sometimes grace burns."

~

A wealthy Scotsman, who had never had time for church and was on his death bed, sent for the minister. "Meenister, if I left a large sum to the Kirk do you think it would help me over yonder?" The Meenister said, "It would do no harm to try."
—*David MacLennan, Church Chuckles.*

~

GROWTH
(MATURITY)

Mark Twain wrote of a museum in Havana which had two skulls of Christopher Columbus—one when he was a boy and—one when he was a man.

~

Growing old is inevitable; growing up is optional. — *Anonymous.*

~

A little girl fell from her bed at night and explained her predicament this way:
I guess I went to sleep too close to where I got in.

~

A medieval saint said, "The soul can never rest in things beneath itself."

~

If—indeed—we love the Lord with all our hearts, minds, and strength, we are going to have to stretch our hearts—open our minds and strengthen our souls— whether our years are three score and ten, or not yet twenty.

> **God cannot lodge in a narrow mind.**
> **God cannot lodge in a small heart.**
> **To accommodate God—they must be palatial.**
> —*William Sloane Coffin.*

~

To be a giant and not a dwarf in your profession, you must always be growing.
-- *William Mathews.*

~

Oliver Wendell Holmes used to say that a person's mind, stretched by a new idea, never goes back to its original dimensions.

~

You've got to do your own growing—no matter how tall your grandfather was.
—*Irish proverb*

~

A friend of mine says that every man who takes office in Washington either grows or swells; and when I give a man an office, I watch him carefully to see whether he is swelling or growing. —*Woodrow Wilson.*

~

George Bernard Shaw said that the only person who took him seriously was his tailor. He measured him every time they met. All the rest go on with their old measurements.

Remember how the centipede came to grief? One day it happened to notice how marvelously it was made. It studied itself and grew fascinated over its ability to move first one leg, and then another, and another, and another. It began to meditate on how it might become an even better centipede until the day it lay distracted in the ditch and was eaten by a bird.

~

Growth is the only evidence of life. —*John Henry Newman.*

~

I received military training in my youth. I never dreamed of such a thing as a warless world either as a fact or an ideal. I can recall applauding Judge Tourget in a public session at the high school when one morning with resounding phrases, he told us two things. First, civilization was founded on The Ten Commandments and the Sermon on the Mount. Second, that we ought to have a war once every thirty years for the moral tone of the nation. I saw nothing contradictory in those two things and loudly applauded. I have had to go through a complete revolution from that old ethical and psychological attitude in order to stand where I do now, and it took the tragic experiences of the Great War to complete the process.—*Harry Emerson Fosdick.*

~

A little boy graduating from the first grade said to his teacher with tears in his eyes, "I sure wish you knew enough to teach us in the second grade!"

~

It's not a matter of growing old; it's getting old if you don't grow. — *Anonymous.*

~

After a stimulating concert, a woman approached the Polish pianist Paderewski, raving that he was a genius. "Thank you," Madam, he said, "but for many years, I was a drudge."

~

When you were a kid you played: *What do you want to be when you grow up?* Your imagination ran wild, and you came up with neat ideas like being the Good Humor Man and having ice cream bars for breakfast. This game was recycled at a party attended by a friend recently where guests were asked to print on slips of paper what they'd like to be when they really grew up. The slips were unsigned. Here are some of the insights found in the adult version of:

What do you want to be when you **really** grow up.

I'd like to …

...*Be able to throw all these damn masks away.*
... *Allow myself to get angry without feeling guilty.*
... *Trust the running of the universe to God and try not to upstage Him.*
... *Be able to cry when it hurts.*
... *Say "no" to my kids and stick to it.*
... *Make peace with death now at 29 so I don't have to waste time on it for the next 40 or 50 years.*
... *Be able to go to an art exhibit or ballet with my wife and not feel*

like a damn fool.
... Laugh at myself more often.
... Be able to pray again.
... Say "No" to demands upon me that destroy my inner peace.
... Be able to give my kids less affluence and more of me.
... Take as good care of my body as I do of my car.
... Tell people the nice things I often think of them but too seldom say.

Muriel Anderson , "Milwaukee Magazine".

~

Even though you are on the right track, you'll get run over if you just stand there.— *Howard Kirksey.*

~

If you are planning for one year, grow rice. If you are planning for twenty years, grow trees. If you are planning for centuries, grow individuals. — *Chinese proverb.*

~

Anyone who says he played better golf at 55 than he did at 25, wasn't very good at 25. — *Bob Brue, golf pro.*

~

One can count the number of seeds in an apple, but one cannot count the number of apples in a seed. — *Llandridod Wells , "Church Magazine".*

~

The average American today is one inch taller and 25 pounds heavier than in 1960. — *National Public Radio (10-28-2004).*

~

A priest, retiring after forty years of ministry, was asked what he had learned after hearing confessions for all these years. He thought for a moment and said, "I've learned two things. First, most people are not as happy as they pretend to be. Second, most of us never really grow up."

~

The thing that is really hard, and really amazing, is giving up on being perfect and beginning the work of becoming yourself.—*Anna Quinlen, Journalist.*

~

A little girl pleaded with her mother to let her stay up and attend the cocktail party about which she had heard so much. It sounded like such a wonderful party and she knew many of the guests who would be coming. Her mother's constant reply was, "Honey, you're just too young! Cocktail parties are for grownups." But after many tears and much pleading, the mother agreed to let her sit on the stairway and watch for a few minutes as the adults had their party. The next morning, the mother asked, "Well, Honey, what do you think of grownup parties? Her daughter said, "It kind of sounded like riding on the school bus."

~

Heaven

"WELL, I THOUGHT IT COULDN'T HURT TO STAY IN SHAPE."

~

Early in his ministry, Billy Graham arrived in a small town to preach. He asked a little boy where the post office was. When the boy told him, Doctor Graham thanked him and said, "If you'll come to the Baptist Church tonight, I'll tell you how you can get to heaven." The boy said, "I don't think I'll come, Mister. You don't even know how to get to the post office."

~

You don't want no pie in the sky when you die. You want something here on the ground while you're still around.—*Muhammad Ali.*

~

I never saw a moor—
I never saw the sea—
Yet know I how the Heather looks and what a wave must be.
I never spoke with God nor visited in heaven—
Yet certain am I of the spot as if a chart were given.

--*Emily Dickinson.*

~

After losing touch for several months, two friends met on the street. "How's the wife, John?" John was surprised that his friend hadn't heard about his wife's death. "Oh, she died and she went to Heaven. "His friend, terribly embarrassed exclaimed, "John! No! I'm terribly sorry to hear that! Well—actually—I'm not sorry she died and went to Heaven. Uhh...John! That's not exactly what I meant to say. I'm really glad she died and went to Heaven. Uhh —actually—what I really mean to say is—I'm surprised!"

The maid, who was overworked and needed a rest from her labors, pictured herself going to heaven this way:

I'll be where loud anthems is always a ringin'
But as I've no voice, I'm cleared of the singin'.
Don't mourn for me now. Don't mourn for me, never.
I'm gonna do nothin' forever and ever.
--R.J. McCracken, *"Presbyterian Outlook."*

~

A couple was killed in an automobile accident the day before they were to be married. They asked St. Peter at the pearly gates if he could arrange a marriage for them as soon as possible. St. Peter said that would be no problem. But 100 years went by, and they gently reminded St. Peter of his promise. Peter said, "I'm really sorry. We're still waiting for a minister."

~

When she died and went straight to heaven, she could hardly contain her enthusiasm. "This is the most beautiful place I have ever seen! And look at all the people! Why—there's my family! Praise God! Oh—this is wonderful—wonderful!" St. Peter said nonchalantly, "You could have been up here ten years ago if you hadn't eaten all that whole grain cereal."

~

A little boy was walking down the beach with his mother, when they came upon a dead seagull. The little boy asked his mother what had happened to it. "Oh—it died and went to heaven," she replied. "So," her son exclaimed, "God threw it back?"

~

In heaven—an angel is nobody in particular. —*George Bernard Shaw.*

~

A man appeared before St. Peter who inscribed his name in the book of life, and then said, "Welcome! You are now exempt from titles, tags, and taxes."

~

Sam Bartlett, who had been dead for several years, meets his friend, Captain Stormfield, and talks to him about heaven:

Now you just remember—this heaven is as blissful and lovely as it can be, but it's just the busiest place you ever heard of. There ain't any idle people here after the first day. Singing hymns and waving palm branches through all eternity is pretty when you hear about it from the pulpit but it's as poor a way to put in valuable time as a body could contrive. It would just make a heaven of warbling ignoramuses, don't you see? Eternal rest sounds comforting from the pulpit too. Well—you try it once—and see how heavy time will hang on your hands! Why—Stormfield—a man like you,...active and stirring all his life, would go mad in six months in a heaven where he hadn't anything to do. Heaven is the very last place to come to rest in, and don't you be afraid to bet on that!" —Mark Twain, Captain Stormfield's Visit to Heaven.

A Sunday School teacher asked her class if they knew where God lived? One little boy stood up and said, "He lives in Heaven." The teacher asked Prissy if that was correct. "No, Ma'am," Prissy said, "He lives in our bathroom." The teacher was incredulous. "That's right," Prissy went on. "Every morning my Dad stands outside the door and knocks—then shouts: My God—are you going to be in there all morning?"

~

Heaven is where the police are British, the mechanics are German, the cooks are French, the lovers are Italian and the whole place is organized by the Swiss. Hell is where the police are German, the cooks are British, the mechanics are French, the Lovers are Swiss, and the whole place is organized by the Italians.

~

A little girl returned home from Sunday School in tears. Her mother asked her what went wrong. She said, "The teacher asked us, '*How many of you want to go to Heaven?*' Everybody raised their hand. But—Mama—you told me to come straight home."

~

If you read history—you will find that the Christians who did the most for the present world were those who thought most of the next: the Apostles themselves, who began the conversion of the Roman Empire; the artists and intellectuals of the Renaissance; the evangelicals who abolished the slave trade—all left their mark precisely because their minds were occupied with heaven. When Christians have thought little of the other world, they—then—have become ineffective in this. Aim at heaven and you will get earth thrown in. Aim at earth—and you will get neither.—C.S. Lewis.

~

His face was red, his tongue was hanging out, and his halo askew on his head as he jogged past two gentlemen reclining on a cloud. One said to the other, "I don't understand Armstrong. Why would he want to watch his weight and jog now?"

~

Gertrude and Gretchen were inseparable friends on earth. As they grew older—each vowed should she precede her friend in death she would do her utmost to make contact. Gertrude died. Gretchen impatiently waited for some sign that Gertrude was trying to reach her. One night—she sat straight up in bed with the unmistakable conviction that Gertrude was there. Gretchen hollered out, "Gertrude—Gertrude—is that you?" She waited; then her voice was heard, "Yes, Dear. Yes—it's I." Gretchen was so excited. "Gertrude—it is so good to talk with you. I've missed you so much. Tell me—what's it like?" Gertrude replied, "Well—we get up in the morning—we have sex—and we eat lettuce; then we have sex and eat more lettuce..." Gretchen interrupted. "Is that what heaven is like?" Gertrude laughed. "No...actually— I'm a rabbit in Minnesota."

~

HOLY SPIRIT

Someone asked Dwight L. Moody if he had been filled with the Holy Spirit? He said, "Yes, but I leak."

~

The popular actor, Danny Thomas, told of a young boy who was being questioned for Confirmation by his Bishop. "My boy," said the Bishop, "what is the Trinity?" The young fellow had a speech defect, but nevertheless answered, "Father, Son, and Holy Spirit." The Bishop leaned closer saying, "I couldn't understand." The bright youngster responded, "You're not supposed to understand, it's a mystery."

David MacLennan, Church Chuckles.

~

Dr. Fred Craddock, of the Candler School of Theology, says he's not worried by those who sleep during the sermon. He once held a conversation in the Kansas City Airport with a clinical psychologist who had just published an article on the influence of doctors' and nurses' conversations on patients during surgery. The psychologist explained that, if the medical team is buoyant and hopeful in their conversations during surgery, then the patient is buoyant and hopeful during post-operative care. On the other hand, if their conversations are solemn and involved in depressing talk, the patient tends to be depressed and dejected during recovery. Craddock advised:

> *Just keep preaching positively—perhaps the Holy*
> *Spirit will nudge the sleeper during the week.*
> *--Fred Craddock. "Sprunt Lectures", Union Seminary (02-1991).*

~

Stanley Bing, writing on his spiritual quest, says, "I tried to catch the Buddhism wave for a couple of days. It didn't really work. You have to sit for hours and hours and think about nothing. I normally get paid for that. And there are no guarantees such contemplation will pay off in anything more than a certain quiet satisfaction. Me, I'm looking for ecstasy. So I moved on."

—"Fortune Magazine", (11-10-1997).

~

> *God did not give us a spirit of timidity,*
> *but a spirit of power and love and self-control.*
> *—II Timothy: 1:7*

~

What is the chief end of man?—To get rich. In what way?—Dishonestly if we can; honestly if we must. Who is God, the one and only true God?—Money is God, God and Greenbacks and Stock—father, son, and ghosts of the same, three persons in one; these are the true and only God, mighty and supreme."

Mark Twain, "The Revised Catechism, New York Tribune," (09-27-1871).

~

James Atwood

A friend of mine was educated in a Catholic high school in Quebec where the nuns often chaperoned the dances. When the students would dance *too close*, one of the nuns would walk by, tap them on the shoulder and say, "Leave room for the Holy Ghost."

~

One Sunday morning, one of my members announced that if anyone wanted to learn how to speak in tongues, she would teach them how.

~

The Doctrine of the Trinity

Discloses partiality in leaving out of Deity
all trace of femininity.
One of the three should be a She.

The writers of theology are strong on masculinity; their doctrine of the Trinity
Reflects their sex, not God's, you see.
One of the three should be a She.

The manifest Divinity required a real nativity and that required maternity,
And a woman's creativity.
One of the three should be a She.

If adding femininity upsets God's unanimity, just rest assured; two out of the three
Comprise a strong majority.
One of the three should be a She.

Which one of the three should be a She? We recommend this Trinity:
Because the Cosmos needs a hostess
It will be Father, Son and Holy Ghostess.

—*Robbins Ralph, "The Women of the Episcopal Diocese of Pittsburgh, P.A."*

~

A woman was ill and couldn't attend church. She sent her nine year old son and instructed him to listen carefully and tell her what the sermon was all about. On returning home, he told his mother that the subject was, "Don't worry, you'll get the quilt." She asked him to repeat that, which he did, but she was unable to get any meaning from it. Puzzled, she called the preacher and asked him to tell her the subject of the sermon. He replied that his key text was, "Fear not. The Comforter will come."

~

54

HUMANKIND

How far can the Brave New World go? It won't be long before every large company will have four or five robots roaming about the premises inspecting things and walking and talking like human beings. But my bet is there will always be a human backup, at least one in a glass case on each floor, which the robots can break in case of emergency.

~

All that I care to know is that a man is a human being-- that is enough for me; he can't be any worse. *--Mark Twain.*

~

Sometimes we forget who we are and what we're here for. Consider the epitaph:

> **Here lies Thomas Livingston.**
> **Born a man.**
> **Died a wholesale grocer.**

~

Santayana said, "Man's oddity is his interest in things not edible."

~

Nicholas Murry Butler, former President of Columbia University, once observed that people can be classed into three major categories. There is a small group of people who make things happen. There is a somewhat larger group of people who watch things happen.   And there is an overwhelming majority of people who don't have the slightest idea at all what is happening.

-- Marlene Wilson, The Effective Management of Volunteer Programs.

~

Man is the only animal that blushes or needs to. —*Mark Twain.*

~

When there are two conflicting versions of a story, the wise course is to believe the one where people appear at their worst. —*H. Allen Smith.*

~

Any system that depends on human reliability is unreliable. —*Tom Gilb.*

~

Our ignorance of history makes us libel our own times. People have always been like this. —*Gustave Flaubert.*

~

Man is equally incapable of seeing the nothingness from which he emerges and the infinity in which he is engulfed. —*Blaise Pascal.*

Man: An animal [whose] chief occupation is the extermination of other animals and his own species, which, however, multiplies with such insistent rapidity as to infest the whole habitable earth and Canada. —*Ambrose Pierce.*

~

Man is more of an ape than many of the apes. —*Friedrich Nietzsche.*

~

Our humanity is a poor thing, but for the divinity that stirs within us.
—*Francis Bacon.*

~

Two things are as big as the man who possesses them, neither bigger nor smaller. One is a minute, and the other is a dollar. —*Channing Pollock.*

~

We are all in the gutter, but some of us are looking at the stars. —*Oscar Wilde.*

~

Man is a reasoning rather than a reasonable animal. --*Alexander Hamilton.*

~

People are very odd creatures; One half censure what they practice, the other half practice what they censure; the rest always say and do as they ought.
—*Benjamin Franklin*

~

I believe our Heavenly Father made man because he was disappointed in the monkey. —*Mark Twain.*

~

I am the inferior of any man whose rights I trample under foot. Men are not superior by reason of the accidents of race or color. They are superior who have the best heart-- the best brain. The superior man. . . . stands erect by bending above the fallen. He rises by lifting others. --*Robert Green Ingersoll.*

~

President George Walker Bush visited a Washington, DC nursing home where he shook hands with one of the residents and asked, "Do you know who I am?" The man replied, "No, I don't. But if you ask one of the nurses, they can help you."

~

A group of British soldiers got lost in the desert during the Gulf War. They eventually stumbled across an American Five-Star General who was surveying the field. "Do you know where we are?" the men blurted out. The general, annoyed that they were improperly dressed and didn't salute or address him correctly, asked them if they realized just who he was. "Now we've got a real problem," said one of the soldiers. "We don't know where we are, and he doesn't know who he is."—*Anonymous.*

~

We're all worms, but I do believe I'm the glow worm. --*Winston Churchill.*

~

JESUS

"SOME TIMES I DON'T UNDERSTAND JESUS. HE NEVER SEEMS TO WANT TO KICK BUTT"

A tackle on the Liberty College Football Team said, "Jesus would have been a great football player. He would have put people on their butts."

~

Jesus was a Jew yes: but only on his mother's side.—*Stanley Ralph Ross.*

If you, General Bertrand, do not perceive that Jesus Christ is God very well: then I did wrong to make you a General.—*Napoleon.*"

~

I think I have a pretty good fix on Jesus," said the preacher. He should be careful. Many folks have been quite surprised by Jesus—especially his disciples—who lived in his bodily presence for three years and often said:

We don't know what He's talking about. -- *John: 16:18*

"Who can tell me what Easter is?" asked the Sunday School teacher. Here are some of the answers the children gave her:
It's when you eat a lot of turkey and are thankful.
It's when you give presents to people because of the birth of the baby Jesus.
Easter is when you send cards with hearts on them to people you love.
"These are all wonderful holidays," the teacher said, "but Easter is really special. Is there anyone else who might know what Easter is?" A little girl raised her hand: *Easter is when Jesus was killed on a cross and was buried. But then, he came back to life again. The stone was rolled away from the tomb— BUT—when Jesus saw his shadow he went back into the tomb for another six weeks.*

When Perry Smith played cornerback for the Green Bay Packers, he had a conversion experience and dedicated himself to the Lord. He vowed that he would, "...play every down just like Jesus Christ would if He were playing left-cornerback." How the Lord Jesus would play cornerback is an intriguing question! But at least on punt situations—Smith tells us his assignment. "I'm to rush the kicker, then hustle back and look for an opportunity to cream somebody."

—*"The Presbyterian Outlook".*

~

The rector of a small church in Los Angeles told of an unkept man who dropped by his church every day at 12:00 noon. The rector asked if he needed anything. He replied, "No, I just come and stand before the altar and offer the only prayer I know. I say, *Jesus—it's Jim.* It's not much, but I think God knows what I mean." Some time later, the priest had a call from an order which served the indigent. The nun told him that Jim had changed the entire atmosphere of the care facility. She had asked him, "Jim—how is it that you are able to bring such joy and peace to these men?" Jim told her, "It's because of my visitor. Every day at 12:00 noon he comes and stands by my bed and says, *Jim—it's Jesus.*"

~

A mother was preparing pancakes for her two sons. The boys started arguing over who would get the first pancake. The mother saw this as a good teaching moment and said, "If Jesus were sitting here, He would say, 'Let my brother have the first pancake, I can wait.'" The older brother turned to his younger brother and said, "Okay, you be Jesus."

~

Former St. Louis Cardinal Manager, Whitey Herzog, was disappointed with the all-around performance of his veteran catcher, Darrell Porter. When Porter took ten fastballs while striking out four times in one night, Herzog told him: "Darrell, you've got to do better than that!" A born-again Christian, Porter reassured Herzog that the Lord was with him. "You better listen to me, Herzog replied. "The Lord's a terrific guy, but he doesn't know anything about hitting." — *"Chicago Tribune."*

~

Despite our efforts to keep him out, God intrudes. The life of Jesus is bracketed by two impossibilities: a virgin's womb and an empty tomb. Jesus entered our world through a door marked "No Entrance" and left through a door marked "No Exit."—*Peter Larson, "PRISM Magazine" (Jan/Feb 2001).*

~

At the graduation exercises at Davidson College, a Presbyterian School in North Carolina, the valedictorian was making his way to the podium and everybody was settling back in their seats to hear what he would say to the gathered assembly. He said, "Many years ago, our Lord Jesus said, ...*love one another.* I have nothing significant to add." Then he sat down. The next day, the *"Charlotte Observer"* commented, "The young man could have done better than that." Could he?

~

NEIGHBOR

"AM I MY KEEPER'S BROTHER?"

A new resident was introduced to the other apes in the ape house at the Washington Zoo. They were rather cool at first. But one finally asked, "Who are you anyway?" The new ape replied, "According to the zoologist, I'm my keeper's brother."

~

Remember that poignant scene in *The Fiddler on the Roof* where the beggar asked for alms? Tevyah gave him one kopeck. The beggar remarked, "Last week you gave me two." Tevyah replied, "Well, I had a bad week?" The beggar said, "So, you had a bad week? Why should I suffer?"

~

I had a neighbor who got angry that my dog barked, but he had no clue that loud rock music could be a problem for me.

~

A good neighbor is better than a far-away friend. —*Dutch proverb.*

~

The Day of Atonement atones for offenses of man against God, but it does not atone for offenses against man's neighbor, till he reconciles his neighbor.
—*Jewish Mishnah.*

~

When your neighbor's house is afire your own property is at stake. —*Horace.*

~

Many a servant of good causes in his community, who seriously proposes the abatement of some social nuisance or moral plague, is surprised at the hornet's nest of antagonism he arouses. General Booth of the Salvation Army, once said, "The day has gone when the priest and Levite are content to pass by the wounded man. They want to turn back and punch the head of any good Samaritan who dares to come to the rescue."—*Harry Emerson Fosdick, The Meaning of Service.*

~

We used to be a society of people who depended on our neighbors and didn't worry much about strangers. Today, we are a society of people completely dependent on strangers and we don't worry much about our neighbors.—*Anonymous.*

~

A man fell into a pit and couldn't get out. His predicament elicited the following comments:

> **A sympathetic person***: I feel for you down there.*
> **An objective person***: It's logical that someone would fall down there.*
> **A self-righteous snob***: Only bad people fall into a pit.*
> **A Calvinist:** *Endure the pit to the glory of God.*
> **A Charismatic:** *Praise the Lord and you won't even know you are in a pit.*
> **A self-pitying person:** *You haven't seen anything until you've seen my pit.*
> **An optimist***: Things could be worse.*
> **A Pessimist***: Things will get worse.*

A Christian took him by the hand and lifted him out of the pit, and said:

> **I'll take care of you until you recover.**

~

Carl Sandburg was asked, "What is the most terrible word in the English language?" After considerable thought, he replied, "Exclusive."

~

Poor neighbors can't hear their own dogs bark.

~

Will Rogers was invited to say a few words at a church service in Canton, Ohio, which boasted of the biggest Sunday School in the United States. In his words:

> *Well, I did, and it seemed to be going pretty good, nobody was converted, but everybody seemed to be laughing. When I would stop, the minister would tell me to go on, and I kept going on … me hesitating and him encouraging me to go on … until when I finished, he didn't get up and preach at all. I had preached and didn't know it. That preacher just used me to conserve a sermon of his that morning, or else he didn't have one. But I enjoyed it, and the church audience applauded. I think it made me better, for on my way back to the hotel I passed a beggar selling lead pencils, and I know I passed him with more feeling and kinder wishes than before. If I didn't write with a fountain pen, I could have helped him.*

~

A bear was chasing two men and closing the gap. When the bear was about 200 yards away, one of the men stopped to tie his shoes. The other said, "You're crazy, stopping to tie your shoes like that. You can't outrun that bear anyway." He looked up and said, "I don't need to outrun the bear. I just need to outrun you."

We make our friends,
We make our enemies, but—
God makes our next door neighbor.
.—*G.K. Chesterton*

~

Some people are so near sighted that they can't see the need for charity until they're up against it. —*Anonymous.*

~

Carlyle tells of an Irish widow who in Edinburgh with three children sought help in vain, fell ill of typhus and, infecting seventeen others, died. "The forlorn Irish widow," cries Carlyle grimly, "appeals to her fellow creatures, *Behold, I am sinking bare of help. I am your sister; one God made us. You must help me.* They answer, *No! Impossible: You are no sister of ours!* But she proves her sisterhood; her typhus kills them; they actually were her brothers and sisters—though denying it."

~

Have you ever wondered if we are here to help others, why are others here?

~

A man and his wife were awakened at 3 o'clock in the morning by a loud pounding on the door. A drunken stranger, standing in the rain asked for a push. "Not a chance," says the husband. "It's three o'clock in the morning!" He slams the door and returns to bed. "Who was that?" asked his wife. "Just some drunk asking for a push," he answers. "Did you help him?" she asks. "No, I didn't. It's three in the morning and it's pouring out." His wife suggested he had a short memory. "Can't you remember? About three months ago when we broke down and those two guys helped us? I think you should help him and you should be ashamed of yourself." The man, feeling guilty, gets dressed, and goes out into the pouring rain, calling out in the dark, "Hello, are you still there? Do you still need a push?" calls out the husband. "Yes, please!" comes the reply. "Where are you?" asks the husband. "Over here—on the swing," replies the drunk.

~

There was once a rabbi in a small Jewish village in Russia who vanished every Friday morning for several hours. The villagers used to boast that during these hours their rabbi ascended to heaven where he talked with God. A skeptical newcomer determined to find out just where the rabbi really went. One Friday morning he hid near the rabbi's house, watched him rise, say his prayers and put on the clothes of a peasant. He saw him take his axe and go into the forest, chop down a tree, and gather a large bundle of wood. Then he proceeded to a shack in the poorest section of the village in which lived an old woman and her sick son. He left them wood which was enough for a week. Then he returned to his own house. The newcomer became a disciple of the rabbi. And whenever he heard one of the villagers say, "On Friday morning our rabbi ascends to heaven to talk with God", he quietly added, "if not higher, if not higher." —*Anonymous.*

~

PAIN
(SORROW)

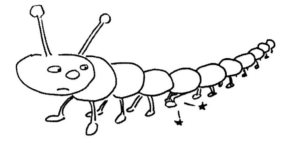

"IF YOUR FOOT HURTS, YOU HURT ALL OVER"

--Sign in a North Carolina shoe store.

~

The Judge asked the man in Traffic Court why he had parked in front of a fire hydrant that was plainly visible. He responded, "Your Honor, I was having some root canal work done. I knew when I parked there it was illegal, but I thought if I could worry about getting a ticket, it would help me get my mind off the pain."

--Unknown

~

God whispers to us in our pleasures, He talks to us in our daily routines, but God shouts to us in our pains. —*C.S. Lewis.*

~

There was a faith healer of Deal, Who said, "Although pain isn't real, When I sit on a pin, and it punctures my skin, I don't like what I fancy I feel.

— Anonymous.

~

I had a broken elbow and was sent to the physical therapist to speed the healing process. The first 20 minutes of my visits were wonderful. I enjoyed a nice hot whirlpool and had an electric pulsating current applied to my arm with some deep heat. It was so nice I used to fall asleep on the table. That was followed by more deep heat treatment and a soothing massage. But having been comforted, the therapist began to stretch me and pull me, and push me so that I winced and frowned and moaned and cursed. But comfort is meaningless unless you're stretched.

~

"I no longer look at life through my glasses, but through teardrops."

—Grieving mother

A cardiologist friend asked one of his patients to describe her heart attack. She said, "Doctor, it just felt like an elephant was sitting right on my chest. But, when I looked, there was no elephant there."

~

Approached by one of his freshman students and asked if he could offer him some advice, William Sloane Coffin said, "Go ahead." The student began, "Well, Sir, when you say something that is both true and painful, say it softly. In other words," he counseled, "say to heal and not to hurt. Say it in love."

~

As a child, if I started to play the *If-Only game*, my Dad would bring me back to reality by saying, "If only a bullfrog had wings he wouldn't bump his tail when he lands."

~

Any stone in your boot always migrates against the pressure gradient to exactly the point of most pressure. —*Milt Barber.*

~

Those who do not feel pain, seldom think that others feel it.
—Samuel Johnson.

~

One day, when our son, David, was 14, my wife came home to hear him crying upstairs in his room. My wife went to him and found his ashen face wet with tears. He told of events that afternoon while he was playing in the back yard of his best friend's home. The boys had found a long rope which they threw over a branch of a tree and then took turns pulling one another up high so they could look out over the neighborhood from this lofty perch. When John's turn came, the rope was almost worn through and as he reached the top of the tree the rope broke and he fell to the ground, crushing his leg beneath him. As he lay in agony on the ground with the bone protruding, all the boys could do was call for help and stand by watching their friend in pain. My son said, "Mother, I couldn't do anything to help. There was nothing I could do to help John."

~

The Scottish Presbyterian Church once banned anesthesia for its women members who were in labor believing that pain in childbirth was God's will.

~

Whenever I need a shot of Novocain, my dentist rather clumsily turns his back toward me, holding a huge needle, so I will not be alarmed. Then he says soothingly, "You're going to feel a small stick.

~

" No pain—no gain.
—*Sports adage.*

~

In Love's Army, only wounded soldiers can serve.
—*Unknown.*

Those who don't know how to weep with their whole heart don't know how to laugh either. —*Golda Meir.*

~

Eyes that will not weep make other organs cry.— *Anonymous.*

~

In the Rosehill Cemetery in Chicago, there is an intriguing comment on the grave of Charles DuPleiss:

Now ain't that too bad.

--*Louis Schafer, Best of Gravestone Humor.*

~

When sorrows come, they come not as single spies, but in battalions.

—*William Shakespeare.*

~

A moment of time may make us unhappy forever.

—*John Gay.*

~

All sorrows are bearable if there's bread.

—*Cervantes.*

~

You may forget with whom you laughed, but you will never forget those with whom you wept. — *Anonymous.*

~

I walked a mile with Pleasure;
She chattered all the way,
But left me none the wiser
For all she had to say.
I walked a mile with sorrow
And ne'er a word said she;
But, oh the things I learned from her
When sorrow walked with me.

— *Anonymous.*

~

There are a good many real miseries in life that we cannot help smiling at, but they are the smiles that make wrinkles and dimples.—*Oliver Wendell Holmes.*

~

It is foolish to tear one's hair in grief, as if grief could be lessened by baldness.

--*Cicero*

~

It is in no man's power to have whatever he
wants; but he has it in his power not to wish for
what he hasn't got—and cheerfully make the
most of the things that do come his way.

—*Seneca 4, BCE 65.*

Dr. Carl Menninger, after giving a lecture on mental health, answered questions from the audience. One asked him, "What would you advise a person to do if one felt a nervous breakdown coming on?" To their astonishment, he replied, "I would lock up the house, go across the tracks, find someone in need and do something to help that person."

~

Where there is sorrow, there is holy ground.
—*Oscar Wilde.*

~

Human nature is such that a war in the Middle East, or an earthquake in Pakistan or whatever calamity hits the front page of the newspaper is never quite as painful as a tiny dent on your new car.

~

No man is more unhappy than the one
Who is never in adversity:
The greatest affliction of life
Is never to be afflicted.
--*Unknown.*

~

"We're afraid to be human because if we're human we might get hurt. We live in a society that tells us to take aspirin or Anacin—so there's no pain, whatever we do. We don't grow if we're not open to hurt." —*Madeleine L'Engle.*

~

Ears pierced with or without pain.
—*Sign in Times Square*

~

I doubt that you have ever had a minor operation.
Minor operations are for other people.

~

Charlie Brown is absorbed listening to his record. When Lucy appears, he says, "You know, that song always depresses me. It brings back so many sad memories. Do you know what I mean? I've never heard another song that depresses me the way that one does. After a long pause he says, "Play it again, will you?"--*Charles Shulz, "Peanuts".*

~

There has never been a philosopher who could endure the toothache patiently.
--*William Shakespeare.*

~

I thank God for my handicaps,
For through them I have found myself,
My work, and my God.
--*Helen Keller*

~

James Atwood

PERSEVERANCE*

The twelve year old girl whose job is to mow the grass for her family is learning a lot about life. Someone asked her what was the hardest thing about her work. She replied, "The hardest thing about mowing the lawn is that it never stays mowed."
—Unknown.

~

The person who says it can't be done, should not interrupt the one who is doing it.
–Ming Lo's Law.

~

We put our best foot forward but it's the other one that needs attention.
—*William Sloane Coffin.*

~

There was a chameleon who was a master at changing himself to fit in with his environment which, it seemed, was always changing. He did exceptionally well until the day when he had to cross a plaid dress. He died a hero's death trying to relate to all the colors at once. *--Carl Sandburg.*

~

Winston Churchill was criticized for speaking too long. He announced he was going to heed this criticism, and he vowed that his next speech would be no more than 10 words. When he was invited to speak at the Military Academy in England, bets were made all over the country as to whether he'd keep his promise. When he got to the platform he said:
Never give up. Never give up. Never. Never. Never.
…and sat down.

~

A young jockey in the Fifties lost 250 races before he had a winner. By that time Eddie Arcaro had learned a lot about racing and went on to become the best jockey in the United States.

~

 "You need to be like ice cream," said the father to the son. The boy asked his father what he meant. "You know, it's often licked, but never beaten."

~

"The hero," Emerson said, "is no braver than an ordinary man, but he is brave five minutes longer."

~

"I want to be a good golfer and I'm willing to work at it," said the client to the golf pro. "Now, which club do I use to make holes in one?"

~

Fall seven times. Stand up eight.
--Japanese proverb.

I stopped playing the piano when I was ten years old because my male ego was bruised. I had mastered *The Indian Wigwam Dance* in Thompson's Piano Book. My next assignment was *The Dance of the Blue Fairy*. Regrettably—I said to my self, "Real men don't play tunes about blue fairies." What I'd give to be able to play *The Dance of The Blue Fairy,* today.

~

Every little bit helps. Every little quit hurts.
—*Unknown.*

~

It's not the jumping fences that hurts the horse's feet, it's the hammer, hammer, hammer on the hard highway. –*Old song.*

~

We can do anything we want to do if we stick to it long enough.
--*Helen Keller.*

~

When Robert and Mary Moffat traveled as missionaries to Bechuanaland, they labored for ten years without a single convert. Their directors thought about closing down their work. Just about that time, one of Mrs. Moffat's women friends wrote from England and inquired what gift they could best use. Mrs. Moffat wrote back, "Please send a communion set, it will surely be needed." Finally, six new converts became a part of the first Christian Church in Bechuana. The communion set reached the Moffat's one day before these persons were to receive communion for the first time. --*London Missionary Society.*

~

Life is like riding a bicycle. You don't fall off unless you plan to stop pedaling.
--*Claude Pepper.*

~

The comedian Joey Adams has a marvelous toast: "May all your troubles last as long as your New Year's resolutions."

~

Why do you sit there looking like an envelope without any address on it?
--*Mark Twain.*

~

If two wrongs don't make a right, try three. –*Lawrence J. Peter.*

~

A chicken doesn't stop scratching just because the worms are scarce.--*John Peers.*

~

If people knew how hard I had to work to gain my mastery, it wouldn't seem wonderful at all. —*Michelangelo.*

~

When you get to the end of your rope, tie a knot and hang on.--*Franklin D. Roosevelt.*

~

*See also, Discipline.

POWER

A Naval Officer was assigned to the bridge of a battleship during World War II. The ship was in U.S. coastal waters but, nevertheless, was maintaining radio silence. The Officer noticed a light that was directly in the path of his ship. He instructed those who were manning the light flasher to send a message to them so they would avoid a collision. "Please move." Back came a message. "You move." The officer was perturbed that his order was not obeyed. "Send another message, he bellowed. Move! We are bigger than you are. We are a battleship." Back came another communication."You move! WE are a lighthouse!"

~

Murphy's Golden Rule: *Whoever has the gold, makes the rules.*

~

In a mechanics shop, I saw a picture of a rough, tough looking man. He wore only a loin cloth about his waist. He was unshaven and was eating part of a leg from some creature he had probably ripped off the animal while it was still alive. The caption read, "Even though I walk through the valley of the shadow of death, I will fear no evil because I'm the meanest SOB in the valley."

~

I used to have superhuman powers, but my therapist took them away.

~

Lust of power is the strongest of all passions. —*Latin proverb.*

~

The rooster bragged to all the other animals in the barnyard that he was able to crow up the sun everyday. **"Just watch,"** he said.

~

Never did a prisoner released from his chains feel such relief as I shall on shaking off the shackles of power. —*Thomas Jefferson on his retirement.*

~

Alfred Nobel, who made millions in the manufacture of explosives and was profoundly disturbed by its implications, seemed more in need of a counselor than a new employee. He told the latter, "I wish I could produce a substance or a machine of such frightful efficacy for wholesale devastation that wars should thereby become altogether impossible."

~

A central message of the Christian life is this: ask Jesus for but a thimbleful of help and you get an ocean full in return. —*William Sloane Coffin.*

~

Halford Luccock told of a small old and battered ship that set out from Tampa, Florida to Boston. In the crowd that gathered to see it off, the Captain was taunted that the "old tub" wasn't going to get him very far. "Oh yes, it will," replied the Captain confidently. "Well—what makes you think so?" another disbeliever shouted. "Because—"the Captain answered, "I've got a date with the Gulf Stream."

~

In God's Book, Jesus Christ is called the Lamb. But we don't associate a King's power with a lamb, do we? Neither does the National Football League. It touts Lions, Bears, Bengals, Raiders, Buccaneers, Vikings, Cowboys, Giants and Redskins, but no lambs. Arena Football has no team called The Lambs. No street gang, to my knowledge, is called The Lambs. No car or truck would sell with a name like Lamb. Dodge trucks are ram-tough—not lamb-tough. But in the strange world of the Bible, all creation honors the Lamb that was slain.

~

The USS Torsk, a World War II submarine, is anchored in Baltimore's Inner Harbor as a tourist attraction. A picture of a fish is painted on its bow. What kind of fish? Sunfish? Perch? Bass? Of course not! It is a shark.

~

I was swimming at a beach in Japan, when the lifeguard blew his whistle for a shark alert. No one tarried getting out of the water. Lifeguards don't blow whistles for sunfish alerts.

~

In 1895, the newspapers in New York were debating the wisdom of building a powerhouse at Niagara Falls.

~

My greatest strength is I have no weaknesses. —*John McEnroe*, 1979.

~

John Adams wrote to Thomas Jefferson and pointed to the risks of power. "Power always thinks it has great soul and vast views beyond the comprehension of the weak and that it is doing God's service when it is violating all of God's laws."

~

The aristocrat is sick in bed as four physicians hover over his puny body which is propped up on pillows in a big four-poster bed. One of the doctors checks his temperature and says, "We fear, Mr. Remington, you have picked up a bug from those tenant farmers you threw out of their house this week."

~

Don't force it. Get a larger hammer. — *Anonymous.*

~

The United States Air Force has three of the world's most powerful planes: the F-15, Eagle; the F-16, Falcon; and the F-17, Stealth. Each is designed to accomplish a particular mission—to bring death to the enemy. Each can fly at twice the speed of sound and they represent the ultimate in our air superiority. We speak of them—always—using the phrase air power. But—consider the English sparrow, whose brain is smaller than a pea, who can find a mate, build a nest, and give life to little English sparrows. I never heard of a male F-15 and a female F-15 building a nest and raising little F-15s. Real power is found in the creation of life, not in its destruction.

~

Two Generals, with stars on their shoulders, were appearing before a Senate Investigating Committee. The senior general leaned toward his colleague. "Both of us know that might makes right," he reminded, "but there's no need to belabor it."

~

Dean Sager, formerly of the Washington National Cathedral, tells of a woman who brought her brownie camera to the Cathedral's Easter Morning Worship. National Geographic was featuring the Cathedral in an upcoming issue and arranged for the most modern equipment to synchronize one great electronic flash to capture the splendor of the Easter processional. The woman in the front row focused her brownie camera and clicked the shutter at precisely the instant that the synchronized flash went off with dozens of lights stationed throughout the sanctuary. She shook her camera and looked at it in disbelief, as if to say, "I didn't know I had that much power in this little camera."

~

Almost anyone can stand trouble and adversity. But if you want to know the character of another, put them in a position of power.

~

In the 1990's, PEPCO (Potomac Electric and Power Co.) ran an ad which interviewed children about electricity. They were asked where electricity comes from. One child answered, "The Pilgrims discovered it." Another said, "The Presidents make it." Still another responded, "Benjamin Franklin. That's it, Benjamin Franklin." And finally one child, who was embarrassed as most of us would be if asked the same question, honestly explained, "I don't know. I haven't read that book yet."

~

A Sunday school teacher said to her children, "We have been learning how powerful kings and queens were in Bible times. But, there is a higher power. Can anybody tell me what it is?" One child blurted out, "Three Aces!"

~

A recovering alcoholic told a friend of the strength God gives him so that he can live in sobriety. He said, "I begin every day with the prayer that God will help me resist taking another drink. And every night, I end the day thanking God for giving me the strength to resist. His friend wasn't so sure, and asked him to explain how he could be sure it was God who had given him this strength. "It's got to be God. He's the only one I asked."

~

If some great power would agree to make me always think what is true and do what is right on condition of being some sort of clock and wound up every morning before I got out of bed, I should close instantly with the offer.—*Thomas Huxley.*

~

PRAYER

~

The first time I questioned the power of prayer was attending my first rodeo in Dallas, Texas. A Baptist preacher gave an invocation. "God, protect these brave men from injury". Then these men deliberately chose to climb on huge wild bulls. No one was surprised when some of them got hurt. My question has grown through the years: "Will God protect us when we climb on wild bulls?"

~

Pray to God but keep rowing for the shore. —*Russian proverb.*

~

There is more religion in some people's curses than in other's prayers, especially if the former is sincere and the latter is perfunctory. —*J.W. Mac Gorman.*

~

The animus against foreign aid is not new in American life! When the framers of the Constitution, meeting in Independence Hall in Philadelphia, got bogged down in definition and discussion, Benjamin Franklin suggested they take time out to pray to God for help. "We need no *foreign aid*," Alexander Hamilton answered curtly. —*"Presbyterian Outlook".*

~

I've found that prayers work best when you have big players.
—*Knute Rockne, Notre Dame Football Coach.*

~

In case of nuclear attack, prayer will be restored to the public schools. (Actually, an exam is sufficient.) —*Bumper sticker.*

A CEO who needed some spiritual guidance screamed at the operator, "Damn you. I was listening to Dial-A-Prayer, and you cut me off."

~

The fewer the words, the better the prayer. —*Martin Luther.*

~

I pray on the principle that the wine knocks the cork out of the bottle. There is an inward fermentation and there must be vent. —*Henry Ward Beecher.*

~

Several years ago, Jack Heacock, Pastor of the First United Methodist Church in Austin, Texas, was asked to have the invocation at the Republican Governor's Convention in that city. He prefaced his prayer by saying:

> *Governor Clements, Republican Governors of America, and distinguished guests--before I invoke the presence of God today, I believe it would be proper to level with you about the nature of the God we are asking to be present.*
>
> *The God we address is the mighty Yahweh who took on Pharaoh on behalf of Hebrew slaves and won! The God who took on Herod the Great on behalf of a little Jewish baby and won! This is the God of justice who becomes enraged when power is abused anytime, anyplace in history. This God pays very special attention to the little people of the world and delights in humbling the proud and the mighty. With this bit of understanding who this God is, let us pray.*

~

Prayer is the contemplation of the facts of life from the highest point of view.
                                                                —*Ralph Waldo Emerson.*

~

At a Pastor's Conference, one of my friends was asked to say the blessing at breakfast: *Lord, forbid that today we be like oatmeal—thick, and lumpy, and hard to stir. Help us to be like corn flakes—fresh and crispy and ready to serve.* The next morning, another minister who disliked corn flakes prayed: *O Lord, grant that we may not be like corn flakes—lightweight, brittle and cold; help us to be like oatmeal—warm, filling, and nourishing.*

~

It's no use to ask God with factitious earnestness for A when our whole mind is filled with B. We must lay before him what is in us, not what ought to be in us.
                                              C.S. Lewis, Letters to Malcomb, Chiefly on Prayer.

~

A staff member at *Christian Life* counseled an earnest reader seeking salvation: "We refer you to the Word of God. Start reading the Gospel of John; ask God to make it plain. Then if you have further questions, write us."

Her husband had no use for the Church or things of the Spirit; but on his deathbed, he called his wife, a pillar of the church, to his side. "Polly, you have always had great faith in prayer. I'm afraid I'm dying and if there's anything to it, I want you to pray for me now." Polly immediately dropped to her knees, "O Lord, please have mercy on my poor old drunken husband." At that he stirred. "Damn it, Polly, don't tell him I'm drunk. Tell him I'm sick."

—Richard Walser, "Tar Heel Laughter".

~

"Uncle Pres" Watkins, a hunter and guide, in the western part of North Carolina was leading a group of Presbyterian Preachers up Mount Mitchell when they found themselves in a terrible storm. They gathered to pray for their safety. One asked, "Brother Watkins, wouldn't you like to join us in prayer?" Pres replied, "To tell the truth, preacher, I only know one little prayer and I don't think it would be worth a damn in a storm like this." *—Carl Goerch, "The State Magazine".*

~

"Thousands were in the stands for the Texas-Oklahoma football game. A clergyman was asked to have a prayer. He prayed, "Lord, you know we are not here to pray. Amen."

~

The family hardly ever came to church and all efforts to restore them were futile. But when one day one of the sons, John, was bitten by a rattlesnake, the father sent for the pastor to come and pray for him. This was his prayer:

> *O wise and righteous Father, we thank you, for you have in your wisdom sent this rattlesnake to bite John in order to bring him to his senses. He hasn't been inside the church for years. It's doubtful he has ever before in all his life felt the need for prayer. Now we trust that this will prove a valuable lesson to him and that it will lead to his repentance. And now, Father, we ask you to send another snake to bite Sam, and another to bite Jim, and another big one to bite the old man. We've been doing everything we could for many years but all our efforts couldn't accomplish what this snake has done. We're led to believe that the only thing that will do this family any good is rattlesnakes; so Lord, send us some more. Amen. —"Journal of Religious Speaking".*

~

At age five Thomas Jefferson joined the older children in *The English School*. Disliking school, he slipped away and hid behind an outbuilding, and recited the Lord's Prayer with a request to God that they stop the school. Jefferson was disillusioned by the impotence of his own prayers. He told this story to his grandchildren and perhaps warned them not to expect too much of heaven.

Fawn Brodie, Thomas Jefferson: An Intimate History.

~

Reporting on the Christian Booksellers Convention in Kansas City a few years back, Religious News Service told of a visitor, without an enrollment badge, who was asked how he got in to the display area. He replied:

I knew that the Lord had brought me to Kansas City for this purpose—being the owner of a Christian bookstore in Florida. But, I did not have the money to register. So, I prayed to the Lord for guidance in gaining entrance to the convention. Then I walked all the way around the building, and sure enough, I found that one of the doors on the loading dock had been improperly closed. With a little effort and with help from the Lord, I opened the door and sneaked into the hall. My prayers were truly answered.

~

Paul Scherer in his book, *The Word God Sent*, tells of an anguished little girl. He asked why she was crying. "Somebody has gone and set traps out there for the birds," she moaned, pointing to the bushes that lined the garden path. "What have you done about it?" he asked. "I prayed about it," she answered. "I prayed that none of the birds would go near the traps and, if they did, I prayed that the traps wouldn't work—and—just a few minutes ago," she went on, looking up and smiling through her tears, "I went out there and kicked the traps to pieces!"

~

St. Augustine used to pray, "Oh God, make me chaste, but not yet."

~

The headmaster of a boy's school prayed, "Lord, save us from intellectual arrogance ... which means..."

~

A layman at a Y.M.C.A. public-relations luncheon prayed: "As we proceed with our deliberations, we ask that Thou shalt help us the best You know how."

~

A minister discovered at the last minute that he and his wife had failed to invite one member of the congregation to their garden party. He tried to correct the oversight by telephoning to apologize and to say he hoped that she would be able to come. "It's too late," she replied sharply. "I've already prayed for rain."

—*"United Church Observer"*.

~

A little fellow who was ready for bed interrupted a family gathering in the living room. "I'm going up to say my prayers now. Does anybody want anything?"

~

Pat Kelly was a talented pinch hitter for the Baltimore Orioles. In a cliff-hanger of a game, he hit a pinch hit grand slam home run in the bottom of the ninth to give Baltimore a victory over the New York Yankees. Interviewed after the game, he said, "I want to give all of the honor to the Lord. He was on my side and helped me do it." His manager, Earl Weaver, challenged Pat's theology. He said, "Pat, I don't believe the Lord even cares who hits home runs or strikes out. The Lord didn't hit the home run. You hit it. If you don't blame God when you strike out, don't give God credit when you succeed."

~

RECONCILIATION

More and more these days, I find myself pondering on how to reconcile my net income with my gross habits. —*John Kirk Nelson.*

~

The Day of Atonement atones for offenses of man against God, but it does not atone for offenses against man's neighbor, till he reconciles his neighbor.

—*Jewish Mishnah.*

~

Reading of the struggles to end apartheid, I was moved by an article about Nyameka Goniwe, the widow of a black activist who was killed in 1985 by the South African Government.. The government said at that time that her husband should be, "permanently removed from society as a matter of urgency." High government officials were later put on trial for his death.

~

Mrs. Goniwe, who works in Capetown for the church, said that she would settle for an official admission that the apartheid state used its machinery to kill its opponents. She said, "What could heal me inside is for this government to own up and say 'yes, we did it.' In exchange for that, I'd be willing to forgive and to try for a national reconciliation. I regard that as a challenge. I challenge myself to forgive."

~

Strange to realize how a good dinner and feasting reconciles everybody.
—*Samuel Pepys' Diary.*

~

When Henry David Thoreau was dying, his Aunt Louisa asked him if he had made his peace with God. "I did not know we had ever quarreled," Thoreau replied.

~

The Rabbi was asked by a disciple how one should pray to gain forgiveness. He sent him to observe the behavior of a certain inn keeper before Yon Kippur. The disciple rented a room in his hotel and observed the owner for several days but found nothing out of the ordinary. But on the eve of Yon Kippur he watched the inn keeper take out two large ledgers. From the first book he read off a list of all the sins that he had committed during the year and for which he was sorry and wanted forgiveness. And then from the second book, he read off a list of things that happened to him during the year which, he felt, were unfair and for which God had to assume some responsibility. Then after reading from both ledgers he said, "Now, God, we're beginning a new year. Why don't we both wipe the slate clean and start over. I forgive you. Please forgive me. —*Jewish folk tale.*

~

If you're going to sin, sin against God—not the bureaucracy.
God will forgive you but the bureaucracy won't.
—*Admiral Hyman Rickover.*

~

Graham Greene has one of his characters say, "Don't talk nonsense, Dear. We'd forgive most things if we knew the facts."

~

"It's wonderful since I found God," confessed a woman. "I used to hate my neighbor with a passion. I promised myself I'd never attend her funeral. But, today, I'd be happy to go to her funeral."

~

A city revolted against its ruler. The King set forth to subdue and punish it, and the city hastily requested a pardon. At a distance from the city, the elders came and begged forgiveness. "For your sake," the King said, "I forgive one-half the guilt." At the gates of the city the masses turned out and pleaded for mercy. "For your sake," said the King, "I forgive half the guilt that is left." When he entered the city and found all the little children gathered with song, and dance and joy to appear before him, he exclaimed: "For your sake, I forgive everything!" and the King joined in their celebration.—*Jewish midrash.*

~

REPENTANCE

The true southern watermelon is a boon apart and not to be mentioned with commoner things. It is chief of this world's luxuries, king by the grace of God over all the other fruits of the earth. When one has tasted it, he knows what the angels eat. It was not a southern watermelon that Eve took; we know that because she repented. —*Mark Twain*, Pudd'nhead Wilson's Calendar.

~

The best part of repentance is the sinning. — *Arabian proverb.*

~

Repentance has a double aspect; it looks upon things past with a weeping eye, and upon the future with a watchful eye.--*Robert South.*

~

When George Brett played for the Kansas City Royals he did not understand the meaning of repentance. At one Spring Training game, he grew irritated at a journalist, grabbed his camera and smashed it against a wall. When questioned about the incident, Brett said, "I regret what I did, but I'm not sorry I did it." Is that what you call a fine line? *Associated Presss.*

~

My favorite highway sign: U-Turns Permitted.

~

A man is trying to apologize to his wife after an argument, but she doesn't think his repentance is sincere. She says with a scowl, "You say you're sorry. You might even act sorry. And I admit you look a bit sorry. But you're not really sorry. I can tell."

~

Believe it or not, a man stopped his car next to a boy on the side of the road and asked how far it was to his destination. The boy said, "If you keep on in the direction you're headed, it will be about 25,000 miles. But if you turn around and take your first right, you'll have about three miles to go."

~

After her surgery, Cathy Miller, was given a list of post-surgical exercises. At the end of the list was "Every three hours place both hands firmly over the incision, breathe in, cough deeply, and repent several times." —*"Reader's Digest".*

~

A Christian is a man who feels repentance on
Sunday for what he did on Saturday and is
going to do again on Monday.

--Thomas Ybarra

James Atwood

While riding on a subway in New York City a pastor had his wallet stolen. A couple days later he got a letter in the mail: "Reverend, I stoal youre munny. I didn't kno you was a Reverend. Remauss is noring me, so I send sum of it back to you. When it nors again I will send sum mor." —*David MacLennan, Church Chuckles.*

~

A man was lost on the fringes of The Okefenokee Swamp in Georgia. Seeing a farmer in the distance, he stopped his car and walked across a peanut field for some help. "Sir, I hate to bother you, but could you tell me how to get to Savannah from here?" The farmer took off his hat and scratched his head. After a long pause he pointed East, "You go down here about five, six, maybe seven miles and you'll cross a bridge, then you aahh." He rubbed his chin. Then pointed in the other direction, "No, go back West for about four miles, and you'll see a grove of pecan trees and a red barn and then there's a curve, hmmm, no." He took his hat off, looked the man in the eye and said sadly, "Mister, if you want to go to Savannah, you can't start from here."

~

A housepainter often stretched his paint with thinner to increase his profits. One evening he got religion. The next morning he started to repaint a house he had just *finished*. The owner asked, "What are you doing back here?" He replied, "God told me to repaint and go and thin no more."

~

Sleep with clean hands, either by integrity or washed clean at night by repentance.—*John Donne.*

~

If you are not able to change your mind, you're getting stale. I know some folks who are more stale in their 30's than others in their 80's! Letting yourself get stale, where you are always predictable is a terrible thing to do to yourself, or your marriage. God created you to grow and mature, which requires a change.

~

Repentance has a double aspect; it looks upon things past with a weeping eye, and upon the future with a watchful eye. —*Robert South.*

~

There's nothing lost by discarding your faults. —*Sophia Bedford-Price.*

~

A priest and a pastor stood by the side of the road and pounded a sign into the ground which read:

The End is Near!
Turn Yourself Around Now—
Before It's Too Late!

The driver in a car speeding past yelled, "You religious nuts!" From the curve ahead they heard screeching tires and a big splash. The pastor turned to the priest and suggests: *Maybe we should just say, Bridge Out?*

~

78

RESURRECTION

If one reads the paper and takes to heart what is written on the obituary pages, it's easy to come to the conclusion that the only hope for the world is in resurrecting the dead and burying the living. —*Paul Eldridge.*

~

In one of his travel stories, Mark Twain wrote of a drunk in the catacombs of Rome. When it dawned on him where he was, he exclaimed, "Hallelujah! Resurrection Day, and I'm the first one up!"

~

A fourth grade Sunday School teacher asked her class what they thought Jesus first words were after his resurrection. One little boy raised his hand right away. He threw his hands up over his head and said, "Ta Dah!"

~

In Springfield, Virginia, a family had two Doberman Pinchers. Two houses away lived another family with whom they were great friends. They had a delightful little daughter who just loved dogs and cats, but because of allergies was denied the privilege of having one as a pet. Her parents bought her two fluffy white rabbits with long pink ears, and she was a virtual little mother to them. Everyone on the block marveled at the care she gave her rabbits.

One evening before bedtime, the folks down the street let their Dobermans out to run. In a few minutes, one of them returned with one of Cathy's rabbits in her mouth. It was bloody and dead. What should they do? They didn't have the courage to tell Cathy their dog killed her pet rabbit. Instead, the man took the rabbit to the bathroom, put it in the bathtub, washed it with soap and water and took his wife's blow dryer and dried it. Then he brushed it. After midnight, when everyone was asleep, he tiptoed over to the rabbit shack and put the dead rabbit on the shelf.

The next morning the two neighbors met outside and waited for their carpool to arrive. Cathy's father said, "Paul, the craziest thing has happened. You won't believe this! Yesterday, one of Cathy's rabbits died. So when I got home from work I buried it in the back yard near the fence. This morning it was back in the rabbit shack."

~

A vain little old lady asked her Pastor, "Once you are in heaven, do you get stuck with the clothes you are buried in?"

~

At Easter, all at once we find ourselves in a world of faith in which rainfall and resurrection belong together. From God's point of view the distinction between *natural* and *supernatural*, which has become so familiar to us, does not exist … the rain is no more natural than the resurrection, and the resurrection no more miraculous than the rain. —*Martin Buber.*

~

"Who can tell me what Easter is?" asked the Sunday School teacher. One of the children said, "It's when you eat a lot of turkey and are thankful." Said another, "It's when you give presents to people because of the birth of the baby Jesus." Another said, "Easter is when you send cards with hearts on them to people you love." The teacher said, "You are talking about wonderful holidays, but Easter is really special. Does anyone else know what Easter is?" A little girl spoke, "Easter is when Jesus was killed on a cross and was buried. But then he came back to life again. The stone was rolled away from the tomb." She paused, "But—when Jesus saw his shadow—he went back into the tomb for another six weeks."

~

"Of course, I believe in the resurrection," said the Industrialist, "I see it every afternoon, about 5:00 p.m."

~

Someone wrote a large graffiti on a wall in Grand Central Station in New York City: "Jesus Lives!" Below it, some one wrote, "Does this mean we don't get an Easter vacation?"

~

Winston Churchill planned his own funeral and directed that after the benediction a bugler, standing in the dome of St. Paul's Cathedral, would play taps. That was to be followed immediately by another bugler in the dome who would play reveille.

A Church organist overslept on Easter morning. The sunrise service was scheduled for 6:30 a.m. At 6:31, the minister called to see if she were on her way. She had just gotten out of bed. The following year, early on Easter morning, the Pastor made sure the organist would be on time. At 5:45 a.m. he called and said, "Christ is risen, and you should be too!"

—Cathy Norman, James Weekley, Church Chuckles Two.

~

It is not only earth but heaven, as well, which has a part in today's Paschal Feast. The angels exult, the archangels rejoice, the cherubim and seraphim join us in celebration of today's feast. What room is there for sadness?

St. John of Chrysostom. Easter sermon, (400AD).

~

A letter came from Health and Human Services to a resident in Greenville County, South Carolina: *Your food stamps will be stopped, effective March 1, 1992, because we received notice that you died. God bless you. If your circumstances change, you may reapply.*—S. Bowen Matthews, "Leadership, Summer", (1997.)

~

One of his members was dying and the Rev. Tom Tate was on his way to see her. His daughter, Jessica, said she wanted to send her a picture. Tom was in a hurry and it was nap time, so, she never sent the picture. When Tom told her that the member had died, she responded by saying, "I hope she gets all better real soon." Tom said to his daughter, "Jessica, she is not going to get better, she is dead." Jessica's puzzled look meant it was time to talk again about death, resurrection and heaven with his daughter. After the talk, Tom confessed, her theology was pretty good after all.

~

A man, his wife, and mother-in-law went on vacation to the Holy Land. While they were there the mother-in-law died. The undertaker told them, "You can have her shipped home for $5,000 or you can bury her here in the Holy Land for $150." The man thought for a few moments before he said, "We'll have her shipped home." The mortician asked, "Why? Why would you spend $5,000 to ship her body home, when it would be wonderful for her to be buried here in the Holy Land and you would spend only $150?" The man said, "Look! There was a man who died here about 2000 years ago. He was buried here. Three days later he rose from the dead. I just can't take that chance."—Anonymous.

~

Here lies the body of Solomon Peas,
Under the trees, and under the sod.
But Peas is not here, tis only the pod.
Peas shelled out and went to God.

—Graveyard epitaph.

~

It [the resurrection] is certain because it is impossible. The Son of God died. It is absolutely to be believed, because it is out of place, in poor taste— ineptum, the

Latin adjective is. And was buried, and rose again; it is certain, because it is impossible." —*Tertullian.*

~

I was working on a Lenten sermon with members of the worship committee in the church library which was next to the sanctuary. The text dealt with human suffering and the pervasiveness of evil. As we shared our views we couldn't help but hear a brass ensemble next door practicing for Easter morning. In the background of everything said about evil, pain, and human suffering were the triumphant refrains of Easter. "Jesus Christ is risen today…come, ye faithful raise the strain of triumphant gladness." Aware of the depths, we can also hear the trumpets. That's the way it is.

~

Only where graves are is there resurrection. —*Frederick Nietzsche.*

~

His daughter went to her grandmother's room to wake her up for breakfast and said, "Grandma, wake up! The world's beginning!" —*Halford Luccock.*

~

The stone was moved not to let Jesus out, but to let the disciples in.
—*Bishop G. Ashton Oldham.*

~

William Temple, who became Archbishop of Canterbury, prepped at Rugby, and on the occasion of the reunion of his class, arranged for the old grads to meet in a small town at the foot of a mountain. Temple was the last to arrive, puffing and blowing, perhaps the paunchiest of them all. Fixing the group with his Archbishop's eye he remarked, "Thank God, gentlemen, we do not believe in the resurrection of the flesh." —*"Presbyterian Outlook".*

~

Easter means you can put the truth in a grave but it won't stay there.—*Clarence Hull.*

~

Baptist preacher Carlyle Marney and Methodist theologian Albert Outler had a conversation, one day, concerning resurrection. Marney admitted, finally, that he just couldn't believe in the resurrection all the time. "Why Carlyle," Outler said, "what makes you think you have to believe in the resurrection all the time? You only have to believe in it when someone you love dies or when you come to die."

~

Jesus raised Lazarus from the dead in Bethany, where his home is called:
The House of Laughter.

~

Pat McGeachy's son was experiencing the triumph of the resurrection as he sang his own version of a great Easter hymn. "Up from the grave he arose—with a mighty puff of his toes."—*Pat McGeachy.*

~

SELF

~

A Boomer put her finger on the human dilemma: "It took me twenty-five years of hard work to get to be somebody. But I've just discovered that the person I am really isn't me."

~

The woman most in need of liberation is the woman in every man.

—*William Sloane Coffin.*

~

Someone told Phyllis Diller that she had an inner beauty. Her reply was, "Well, leave it to me to be born inside out."

~

If my theory of relativity is proven successful, Germany will claim me as a German and France will declare that I am a citizen of the world. Should my theory prove untrue, France will say that I am a German, and Germany will declare that I am a Jew. *–Albert Einstein, Address at the Sorbonne..*

~

Individualism is incapable of inspiring anybody. There is nothing great or gripping in it. Individuality can attain its supreme development only in the highest common social order. *–Peter Kropotkin, Russian Philosopher.*

~

We judge ourselves by our motives and others by their actions. *—Dwight Morrow*

There is no true liberty for the individual except as he finds it in the liberty of all. There is no true security for the individual except as he finds it in the security for all. --*Edwin Markham, poet.*

~

Coping with difficult people is always a problem, particularly when the difficult person happens to be oneself. —*Ashleigh Brilliant.*

~

The young man was a picture of confidence as he sat across from the boss who was interviewing him for a position in the company. The Boss inquired, "Tell me, Mr. Tilkens, do you have any other qualifications other than liking yourself and being satisfied with who you are?"

~

.A person is a person through other persons. —*African proverb.*

~

The knowledge of God and that of ourselves are connected. Without knowledge of self there is no knowledge of God, and without knowledge of God there is no knowledge of self. —*John Calvin.*

~

No matter how good you feel, if four friends tell you, "You're drunk," you'd better lie down. —*Proverb.*

~

No one can make you feel inferior without your consent. —*Eleanor Roosevelt.*

~

Everybody has one's own theater in which one is manager, actor, prompter, playwright, scene shifter, bookkeeper, doorkeeper, all in one; and the audience is thrown in as a bargain. —*Julius Hare.*

~

We are so vain that we even care for the opinion of those we don't care for.
—*Maria Ebner-Eschenbach.*

~

At age 20, we worry about what others think of us. At 40, we don't care what they think of us. At 60, we discover they haven't been thinking about us at all.
—*Mike Duduit.*

~

Our business in life is less making something of ourselves than finding something worth doing and losing ourselves in it. —*William Sloane Coffin.*

~

While 54% of the men say they often think of their physical appearance, a much higher 75% of women say the same; and 40% say they spend a lot of time on how they look. The segments of the population who spend the most time tinkering with themselves to look better are young people, those in the highest income brackets, big city residents, residents of the Northeast, the best educated, blacks, singles, and of course, women. But perhaps the depth of Americans' obsession with and insecurity over their looks was revealed when people were asked if they would like to change something about their personal appearance. A nearly unanimous 96% said they would, 94% of all men, and 99% of all women.

—*Louis Harris, "Inside America", (1987).*

~

If I'm not for myself, who will I be? And if I'm only for myself, what am I?

—*Joseph Hillel.*

~

Elia Kazan, one of the most honored and respected directors on Broadway and Hollywood, said of himself, "I'm like a blacksnake. I've shed several skins in my time, lived several lives, and known violent and cruel changes. Generally, I've understood what happened only after it happened."

~

I think I am becoming a God. —*Titus Vespasian, Roman Emperor on his deathbed.*

~

A wild and reckless youth once met Socrates on the streets of Athens and said, "Socrates, I hate you. Every time I meet you, you make me realize what I am."

~

God said, "Build a better world." And I said, "How? The world is such a cold, dark place and so complicated now. And I'm so young and useless, there's nothing I can do." But God, in all God's wisdom, said, "Just build a better you."

—*Max D. Isaacson.*

~

Reverend Jesse Jackson began his work each day with persons in the ghettos of Chicago by having them say, "I am somebody. I am a child of God."

~

Insist on yourself. Never imitate.—*Ralph Waldo Emerson.*

~

Be yourself. Who else is better qualified?—*Frank Giblin.*

~

Look in my face. My name is Used To Was. I am also called Played Out, and Done To Death, and It Will Wash No More.—*Henry Duff Traili*

~

Being a Pastor for many years, I have seen so many who were trying to *find themselves* become the victims of *paralysis by analysis*. Jesus, The Man for Others, gives us some solid advice on finding ourselves. Instead of saying, "Develop yourself", Jesus said, "Forget yourself". Instead of saying, "Actualize yourself," our Lord said, "Deny yourself." Rather than counsel us, "Live for yourself," Jesus said, "Die to yourself and you will find yourself."

~

One theologian reflecting on Hell said, "There's not really any right and wrong. There, it is only what feels good to each individual person."

One cynic said, "I was born a statistic. I live a statistic. And I'll die a statistic!"

~

Be honest, gentlemen. Haven't you ever felt like telling a clerk, "No, I don't want a Tommy Hilfiger shirt. I'm not Tommy Hilfiger. Neither do I want Y.S.L. on my tie. I'm not Yves Saint Laurent. Do you have any ties with my initials, JEA, on them?"

~

Courteous and efficient self-service. —Sign in New York City cafeteria.

~

A local politician sent out a *Dear Neighbor Letter* to thousands of his constituents requesting funds to help in his re-election campaign. When he opened his mail a few days later he was ecstatic. There was a $25,000 check made out to his campaign. He was already planning what he would say to this wonderful friend when he noticed that the check was made out to: *Neighbor.*

~

When an ignoramus goes into a library, he can see only long rows of books, almost indistinguishable as units. But when the librarian comes, the student and lover of books, he knows each one by name. Each volume has its special associations; he knows the edition, the value, the contents, the author, the purpose. He takes down one book after another, revealing his individual appreciation of each. The more he knows as a librarian, the less he sees books in the mass, the more he knows them one by one. —*Harry Emerson Fosdick.*

~

It's difficult to put one's self in proper perspective. The difficulty is compounded when one considers that he or she is $1/4^{th}$ of a family; $1/20^{th}$ of an office staff; $1/450^{th}$ of a church; $1/90,000^{th}$ of a city; $1/280,000,000^{th}$ of a country; $1/5,000,000,000^{th}$ of a world. No wonder some folks consider themselves to be only *the first cousin of an ape that learned how to shave.*

~

Comrades, we must abolish the cult of the individual, decisively, once and for all. —*Nikita Khrushchev.*

~

The shoe that fits one person pinches another; there is no recipe for living that suits all cases. —*Carl Jung.*

~

To your own self be true, and it must follow as the night the day that thou cannot be false to any man. --William Shakespeare

~

Every man has a mob self and an individual self, in varying degrees.
                                                                    --D.H. Lawrence..

~

SELFISHNESS

Where all are selfish, the sage is no better than the fool, just more dangerous.
—*Anonymous.*

~

Abraham Lincoln was walking down the street in Springfield, Illinois with two of his sons who were fighting between themselves. A neighbor inquired what the fighting was about. Lincoln replied, "These boys are fighting just like the rest of the world. I've got five peanuts in my hand, and they're arguing over which one should have three."

~

Selfishness is the only real atheism; aspiration, unselfishness, the only real religion.
—*Israel Zangwill.*

~

Describing the Great Wall of China is like explaining the Grand Canyon. One has to see it to believe it. It is massive and cost an immense amount of money and human lives to build. It seems impregnable, but three times the enemies of China breached it. Not by breaking it down, or going around it, or climbing over it. They did it by bribing the gatekeepers.

~

If you don't believe in original sin, listen to this: "Now I lay me down to sleep. I pray the Lord my soul to keep. And if I die before I wake, I pray the Lord, my toys to break, so none of the other kids can use 'em. Amen."
— *Shel Silverstein, Prayer of a Selfish Child.*

~

If you are all wrapped up in yourself, you're over-dressed. —*Kate Halverson.*

~

Simone de Beauvoir points out in her book on ethics, "If all life does is maintain itself, then living becomes *not dying*, and human existence is indistinguishable from absurd vegetation."

~

"In a period of spiritual bewilderment this year's college graduates have been asked, often in the name of religion, to confuse selfishness with self-reliance, to regard their own government as an enemy, and to concentrate on their own material well-being. My kingdom come … My will be done … Hallowed be my name." —*James Reston, "Reflecting on the Class of '85, New York Times".*

~

Congress just heard that the folks back home don't like a tax increase. In fact, it's three-to-one against. Their lifestyles can't handle it.

~

When American labor presses for equality, they usually mean that they should share more fully in the profits of the stockholders. They do not usually mean that they, in turn, should share their wealth with others who earn less than they. When Management and Labor, both, can see that need, we will have made some social progress. —*Anonymous.*

~

In the 17th Century the central part of London burned down. There was great suffering, but the people were buoyed by the possibility of rebuilding a better and more beautiful London. Sir Christopher Wren drew up the plan which had St. Paul's Cathedral in the very center. The city officials sanctioned the plan, but when they faced the practical details, many people insisted that their houses must be placed exactly as they were before the fire. In the end, a new and better London was not built. They raised the city once again on the same foundations.

~

Everyone is eloquent in his own cause. —*Latin proverb.*

~

The idea of strictly minding our own business is moldy rubbish. Who could be so selfish? —*Myrtle Lillian Barker.*

~

Lord Melbourne is reported to have said, "If we are to have a religion, let us have one that is cool and indifferent such a one as we've got."

~

Coach Nate McMillan charged that Seattle Supersonics center, Jerome James, was selfish. James responded, "I don't have the first clue who he is talking about, because all I do is worry about Jerome." —*"Sports Illustrated", (2003).*

~

I have been a selfish being all my life—in practice, though—not in principle.
—*Jane Austen.*

~

Oysters are more beautiful than any religion. There is nothing in Christianity or Buddhism that quite matches the sympathetic unselfishness of an oyster.
—*Antoine de Saint-Escupery.*

~

The boys started arguing over who would get the first pancake. Their mother, seeing a good teaching moment, said, "If Jesus were sitting here, He would say, 'Let my brother have the first pancake, I can wait.'" The older brother turned to his younger brother and said, "Okay, you be Jesus."

~

The true value of a human being is determined primarily by the measure and the sense in which one has attained liberation from the Self.-- *Albert Einstein.*

~

SERVICE

Every spring when the clocks are moved up for daylight savings time, there are always some people who get to the church just as the closing hymn is sung. Once, a person asked the usher, "Oh, have I missed the service?" The usher, no mean theologian, replied, "Oh, no. Service begins when worship ends."

~

My neighbor bought a new truck. He shines it up more than I shine my shoes. It is a nice truck: beautiful cab, AM/FM, CD, GPS, power windows, etc. I asked him how he liked his truck? "Oh, I love it!" he said. "I bet you can haul a lot of stuff in it," I ventured. He replied, "Well, I haven't carried anything in it yet. I don't want to scratch it up." His remark reminded me of a church which had a gymnasium with a beautiful floor. The officers were so proud of the floor they wouldn't let the kids play basketball on it. They didn't want it to get scratched up.

~

I wish not to preach the doctrine of ignoble ease, but the doctrine of the strenuous life. —Teddy Roosevelt.

~

Every man who says frankly and fully what he thinks, is doing a public service.
--Leslie Stephen.

~

Pressed into service means pressed out of shape. —Robert Frost.

~

Service is the rent each of us pays for living...the very purpose of life and not something you do in your spare time or after you've reached your personal goals.
—Marian Edelman.

~

A florist went to a barbershop to get a haircut. After the cut, he asked about his bill and the barber replied, "I'm sorry, I cannot accept money from you, I'm doing community service this week." The florist was pleased and left the shop. The next morning when the barber arrived at his shop, he found a thank you card and a dozen roses waiting for him at the door. Later, a policeman came for a haircut. When he started to pay his bill the barber again replied, "I'm sorry, I cannot accept money from you, I'm doing community service this week." The policeman left the shop with a smile. The next morning when the barber arrived to open his shop, he found a thank you card and a dozen donuts waiting at the door. Then a Baptist preacher came in for a haircut. When he started to pay his bill the barber again replied, "I'm sorry, I cannot accept money from you; I'm doing community service this week." The preacher was very happy and left the shop. The next morning when the barber arrived to open the shop, he found a dozen Baptist preachers lined up, waiting for their free haircuts!

~

We'll clean for you.
We'll press for you.
We'll even dye for you.
Sign in the window of a dry cleaner.

~

In the film version of *The Royal Hunt for the Sun*, the famous explorer Pizarro and his men are confronted by a deep gorge in the mountains of Peru. Between the two peaks stretches a flimsy rope bridge. Even the bravest among them trembles with fear. Pizarro looks over his disheveled band. In the rear—immobilized with fear and apprehension—stand the clergy. Pizarro issues the summons:

The Church goes first!

~

Doing nothing for others is the undoing of ourselves.
—Benjamin Franklin.

~

Remember Mrs. Jellyby, Charles Dickens' character who wanted to be of use in this world? She was far from unselfish. But her kindness was all related to Borrioboola-Gha in Africa. Her home was a mess; her children were neglected; her most obvious duties were lazily performed so she could shower her concern and attention on those who were thousands of miles away.

~

Service is nothing but love in work clothes.
—Anonymous.

~

A few church members called on an elderly gentleman in the hospital. After a pleasant visit, they assured him that they would be praying for him. He said, "Thanks, but what I really need is to have someone shovel the snow off my sidewalk."

~

A tour group was traveling in Turkey where they visited an asylum and watched a nun clean the main room at the end of the day. It was a messy, dirty job. There was even human excrement caked on the floor. She was on her kneeds scrubbing, and cleaning the room. One of the tourists said in a whisper, "I wouldn't do that for a million dollars." The nun overheard the comment and whispererd back, "Neither would I."

~

The lives of so many people are empty because they have no great purposes, no great hopes, no great commitments, no sense of participation in a great conflict or a great cause. —*H. Richard Niebuhr.*

~

SILENCE

Keep quiet, and people will think you are a philosopher.—*Latin Proverb.*

~

C.S. Lewis in *The Screwtape Letters*, has the Chief Devil say to Wormwood, "Not one little moment of time in Hell will be devoted to silence. You must work to make the whole universe noise."

~

A woman complained to her friend, "You know, Bill never says a word, but his silence is never golden."

~

All the troubles of man come from his not knowing how to be still.
—Blaise Pascal, (1623-1662).

~

To sin by silence when they should protest, makes cowards of people.
--Abraham Lincoln.

~

He has the gift of quiet.—*John LeCarre.*

~

Officiating is the only occupation in the world, Where the highest accolade is silence.—*Earl Strom, N.B.A. Referee.*

~

Errol Garner was a great piano player but he could not read music. When someone reminded him of his limitations, he'd say, "Hell, man, nobody can hear you read."—*Whitney Balliett, "The New Yorker".*

~

George Bernard Shaw once said that America can survive only by some law which would shut up each of us alone in a room for a day each week with nothing to hear or read, so that we would be forced to meditate.

~

"Now children," said the Sunday School Teacher, "I want you to be so still you can hear a pin drop." After a long silence, a little guy in the corner shouted, "O.K. Let 'er drop." —*David MacLennan, "Church Chuckles".*

~

The present state of the world to the whole of life is diseased. If I were a doctor and were asked for my advice, I should reply, "Create silence."
Soren Kierkegaard, "New York Times Magazine", (04-06-1958).

~

All the trouble in the world is due to the fact that man cannot sit still long enough in the quietness of a room. "He must hunt, flirt, chatter, work, or even gamble."
—Blaise Pascal.

Eddie Stanky, former St. Louis Cardinas' Manager, took every defeat to heart. Once in the middle of a losing streak, he went to his favorite barber shop and got a warm welcome from his barber. When asked "How will you have your hair cut, Mr. Stanky?" He replied, "In profound silence please."
—*Herman Masin, "Curve Ball Laughs".*

~

A student once asked Professor Charles Copeland of Harvard why he lived on the top floor of the dormitory. "The rooms are small and dusty. You ought to move." The Professor replied, "No, I shall always live on the top floor. It's the only place where only God is above me. He's very busy, but He's quiet."

~

Better to remain silent and be thought a fool, than to open your mouth and remove all doubt. —*Abraham Lincoln.*

~

Quiet people aren't the only ones who don't say much. —*Howard Kirksey.*

~

Silence is argument carried on by other means.—*Che Guevara.*

~

Blessed are they who have nothing to say and can't be persuaded to say it.
—*J.R. Lowell.*

~

Silence: A conversation with an Englishman.—*Heinrich Heine.*

~

Charlie Brown was pitching and got the batter to hit a lazy fly ball which anyone could have caught. He was jubilant because this sure out meant a win for his team. However, the ball struck Lucy right on top of her head, and the game was lost. Lucy explained, "I was having my quiet time." --*Charles Shulz, "Peanuts".*

~

Silence is golden, we say. But sometimes it is yellow. —*Howard Kirksey.*

~

Never miss a good chance to shut up.—*Will Rogers.*

~

The first sign of maturity is to discover the volume knob turns, also, to the left.
—*Anonymous.*

~

For the most part we are much too busy living and thinking to have leisure to be silent and see. —*Aurobindo, Hindu.*

~

Most of us know how to say nothing. Few of us know **when**. —*Unknown.*

~

Don't talk unless you can improve the silence. —*Vermont proverb.*

~

SIN

"IF IT WEREN'T FOR SIN,"
WE'D BE OUT OF A JOB!

~

Anyone who doesn't believe in original sin has no children.

~

The only business of sin is the extent that it drives the sinner away from his God. Murder is no better than cards, if cards will do the trick.—*C.S. Lewis, The Screwtape Letters.*

~

Sin has many tools, but a lie is the handle that fits them all.
—*Oliver Wendell Holmes, "The Autocrat of the Breakfast Table".*

~

Man has become a new animal who can jump a hundred miles, see through brick walls, bombard the atom, and analyze the stars, yet he goes on behaving like the weak, quarrelsome ape he used to be. —*H.G. Wells, Holy Terror.*

~

Until a child is one year old it is incapable of sin.—*The Talmud.*

~

Today—deviancy is being defined down. —*Sen. Patrick Moynihan.*

~

The Duchess of Buckingham wrote to Lady Huntingdon about the Methodists:
> *Their doctrines are most repulsive and strongly tinctured with impertinence and disrespect to their superiors. It is monstrous to be told*

that you have a heart as sinful as the common wretches that crawl the earth. This is highly insulting and I wonder that your Ladyship should relish any sentiment as much at variance with high rank and good breeding.

~

He conquered by weapons, but was conquered by his vices.
—*Lucius Seneca on Hannibal, the Carthaginian General.*

~

It is in the brain—and in the brain only—that the great sins of the world take place.
—*Oscar Wilde.*

~

Human nature is something that makes you swear at a pedestrian when you are driving and at the driver when you are walking. —*Anonymous.*

~

Our young people are diseased with the theological problems of original sin, origin of evil, predestination, and the like … these are the soul's mumps and measles and whooping cough; and those who have not caught them cannot describe their health or prescribe the cure. —*Ralph Waldo Emerson.*

~

You can no more rid the world of sinners than you can stock it with saints. As Sam Keen warned, "Every utopian scheme hides a Grand Inquisitor."—*William Sloane Coffin.*

~

Most people spend all their lives perfecting their faults. —*Lynn Summer.*

~

If your sins find you *out* why worry! It is when they find you *in* that trouble begins.

~

We moderns don't worry much about our sins, but we do an awful lot of worrying about other people's sins. And—if we are not worried about them—we are certainly worried by them. —*W.B.J. Martin.*

~

The wages of sin are unreported. —*Anonymous.*

~

Describing the Great Wall of China is like explaining the Grand Canyon. One has to see it to believe it. It is massive and cost an immense amount of money and human lives to build. It seems impregnable, but three times the enemies of China breached it, not by breaking it down, or going around it, or climbing over it. They did it by bribing the gatekeepers.

~

I used to be Snow White, but I drifted. —*Bumper sticker.*

There is no original sin. No matter how unusual it is, it has been thought of before by thousands of people. —*"St. Louis Globe-Democrat".*

~

When was the last time the United States of America officially sinned? It was in 1956, when Gary Powers' spy plane was shot down over The Soviet Union. They caught us red-handed, (no pun intended). President Dwight D. Eisenhower in *confessing* the incident before the world, acknowledged that the Russians did have one of our spy pilots, and he used the word—*sin*—to describe our actions. His advisors, The State Department, and several Presidential aides had apoplexy. That was the last time the United States sinned, at least officially. (No succeeding President: Kennedy, Johnson, Nixon, Ford, Carter, Reagan, Bush I, Clinton, or Bush II has used the word *sin* to describe any national activity.)
—*Karl Menninger, Whatever Became of Sin?*

~

A boy asked his older brother after church, "What are sins of omission?" His brother explained: "Those are the sins we should have committed, but didn't."

~

Any time you get a mouthful of hot soup, the very next thing you do will be wrong. —*Anonymous.*

~

The Scriptures tell us that the sins of the fathers will be visited upon the children to the third and fourth generation. Life demonstrates this truth. It also demonstrates that the sins of the children are visited upon the fathers and the mothers.

~

The fall of humankind is really the banana skin joke carried to cosmic proportions.
—*G.K. Chesterton.*

~

My sins are not scarlet, they are gray—all gray. —William Temple.

~

A cautious preacher concluded his sermon: "Any sinners referred to in this sermon are fictitious and any similarity to members of this congregation is strictly coincidental."

~

Sin: that distinguished precipice. —Emily Dickinson.

~

In the early 1900's the London Times invited several well known authors to contribute essays on the topic, "What's Wrong With The World?" A Letter to the Editor was submitted and read:

> *Dear Sirs:*
> *I am.*
> *Sincerely yours,*
> *G. K. Chesterton*

Lord, save me whether I like it or not. Dust and ashes that I am, I love sin.
> —*Prayer of one of the Desert Fathers.*

~

The Seven Deadly Sins are:
> *Politics without principle,*
>> *Wealth without work,*
>>> *Pleasure without conscience,*
>>>> *Knowledge without character,*
>>>>> *Business without morality,*
>>>>>> *Science without humanity,*
>>>>>>> *Worship without sacrifice.*
> —*E. Stanley Jones*

~

The sign in front of the church read:
> **If you are through with sin, come on in.**
Someone added a lipstick graffiti:
> **If not, call 527-4766.**

~

At one year of age, my grandson Woody's most frequent expression is "uh-oh." He spends his days commenting on the things that are not right in his world. When he drops some of his food to the floor, he says "uh-oh." When one of his toys doesn't fit together neatly as it should, he says, "uh-oh." When the room is in disarray, he comments, "uh-oh." When he discovers a piece of material is missing from his nerf ball, he says, "uh-oh." I think he is destined to be a preacher, or perhaps a social critic. But today, he's a precious little boy learning one of life's most important lessons, that the world is chock-a-block full of "uh-ohs." *(1989)*

~

> **Everybody has a little bit of Watergate in him.**
> — *Billy Graham.*

~

A Catholic teenager complained to her priest about waiting so long in line for confession. "There ought to be an express line," she told him, "for those with three sins or less."

~

I haven't yet been able to find a happy adulterer. —*Tamisin Day-Lewis.*

~

There are certain mistakes we enjoy so much we arealways willing to repeat them.
> —*James Geary.*

~

> **Our most destructive sins are two-fold:**
> **Taking ourselves too seriously;**
> **Not taking ourselves seriously enough.**

~

SPIRITUALITY

Spirituality has more to do with serving the homeless than seeking saintliness.

~

"Honk if you love Jesus" is a bumper sticker that calls forth zero spirituality. But, this one does: "If you love Jesus, tithe; anyone can honk."

~

The guest preacher attended a prayer meeting before worship and it went on and on. When it was finally over, the Baptist Deacon asked the guest if there was anything else he could do for him before worship. "Yes, my friend, there is. I've learned over the years that a good sermon requires not only a calm and confident spirit, but an empty bladder. Where's the men's room?"

~

An experienced spiritual director was counseling a society matron who set a goal for herself to think of God the very first moment when she woke up in the morning. For months she worked to establish the habit, but, to no avail. Finally, in the midst of an interminable harangue, the spiritual director gave up. "My dear Madam," she said, "the first thing I think of when I wake up is whether I can get to the bathroom before I wet my pajamas. We are embodied persons."

—"Context".

~

Speaking frankly, to long for the transcendent when you are in your wife's arms is, to put it mildly, a lack of taste, and is certainly not what God expects of us. We ought to find God and love him in the blessings he sends us. If he pleases to grant us some overwhelming earthly bliss, we ought not to try to be more religious than God himself. *—Dietrich Bonheoffer, God's Intention For Man..*

~

At an inter-state college speech contest one young woman, who was very short, checked the microphone and discovered that it was at least a foot above her head. In vain, she tried to adjust it. In a panic she went to the director and blurted out, "The mike's too high. The mike's too high." He replied in a calming voice, "Young lady, you've got ten whole minutes. Now, grow!"

—Kenneth Chafin, "Journal of Religious Speaking".

~

There are only two forces in the world, the sword and the spirit. In the long run the sword will always be conquered by the spirit. *—Napoleon Bonaparte.*

~

It's great to be able to pinch your side and find there's not too much fat. Can you pinch your soul and find the same? *—Christopher Blake.*

One day the learned Rabbi fell on his knees before the ark and in true humility beat his breast saying, "I'm nobody. I'm nobody." The Cantor overheard this humble act of contrition and kneeled beside his spiritual guide, saying, "I'm nobody. I'm nobody." The janitor saw both of his leaders on their knees and quickly joined them saying, "I'm a nobody, too. I'm a nobody, too." Hearing the janitor's confession, the Rabbi nudged the Cantor and said, "Look who thinks he's a nobody." –*Unknown.*

~

Your quest for spirituality is counterfeit and useless if all you do is to soak up *good stuff* like a sponge and never share it.

~

Stanley Bing, writing on his spiritual quest, says, "I tried to catch the Buddhism wave for a couple of days. It didn't really work. You have to sit for hours and hours and think about nothing. I normally get paid for that. And there are no guarantees such contemplation will pay off in anything more than a certain quiet satisfaction. Me, I'm looking for ecstasy. So I moved on."

—*"Fortune Magazine", (11-10-1997).*

~

The spiritual eyesight improves as the physical eyesight declines. —*Plato.*

~

Religion is for people who are afraid of going to hell; spirituality is for people who have been there. —*Anonymous.*

~

Pat Kelly of the Baltimore Orioles was bothered by the profanity of the team manager, Earl (Skip) Weaver. One day he diplomatically said to him, "Skip, I wish you wouldn't talk like that and that you would walk with the Lord." Weaver replied, "Kelly, I'd rather see you walk with the bases loaded."

~

A CEO who needed some spiritual guidance screamed at the operator, "Damn you. I was listening to Dial-A- Prayer, and you cut me off."

~

If it's the religious life you want, you ought to know right now that you're missing out on every single dam religious action that is going on around this house. You don't even have sense enough to drink when somebody brings you a cup of consecrated chicken soup—which is the only kind of chicken soup that Bessie ever brings to anybody around this madhouse. So just tell me, just tell me, buddy. Even if you went out and searched the whole world for a master— some guru, some holy man to tell you how to say your Jesus prayer properly, what good would it do you? How in hell are you going to recognize a legitimate holy man when you see one if you don't even know a cup of consecrated chicken soup when it's right in front of your nose? Can you tell me that? —J. D. Sulinger

~

SUFFERING

A new acquaintance was asked if he went to college. He proudly replied, "I graduated from the University of Michigan. It was a great place for learning. Our colors were blue and gold." After a moment he inquired, "Where did you get your education?" The man replied, "I've been attending the greatest institution of learning there is, but I'll never graduate. It's The University of Life and our colors are black and blue."

~

Jews always know two things: suffering and where to find great Chinese food.
-- "My Favorite Year", movie, (1982).

~

You always know which people have found life a bed of roses. You hear them complaining about the thorns. —Imogene Fey, "Quote".

~

The truth that many people never understand until it is too late is that the more you try to avoid suffering the more you suffer because smaller and more insignificant things begin to torture you in proportion to your fear of being hurt.
—Thomas Merton.

~

In Elie Wiesel's well known memoir, *Night*, from his years in the concentration camp, he tells of being forced to witness an execution of a young man by hanging. As the crowed witnessed the death, out of the crowd came the cry, "Where is God now?" And then the despairing reply, "God is on the gallows."

~

If you suffer—thank God. It's a sure sign you are alive.
—Elbert Hubbard.

~

"My mother burned up in red flames. My sister too burned up in red flames. Only a few ashes remained. Take me back to the past just once more."
--11 year old survivor of the atom bombing of Nagasaki.

~

Master of the Universe, know that the children of Israel are suffering too much; they deserve redemption, they need it. But if, for reasons unknown to me, you are not willing—not yet—then redeem all the other nations—but do it soon.
--Hasidic tale told by Elie Wiesel.

~

One of the most poignant memories I have of Christmas is sitting in Georgetown Hospital with a young mother who watched her energetic two year-old son's strength gradually fade away with a fatal brain tumor. We shed many a tear together as she pleaded and bargained with God. I can still hear her ask, "Will it really help to pray?" I suggested we go to the cafeteria to talk and get a sandwich but we found it difficult to do either. In this agony, we heard in the background:

Deck the halls with boughs of holly,
Fa la la la la la la la la.
Tis the season to be jolly
Fa la la la la la la la la.

~

Miles Laboratories in the magazine, "Psychiatric News," printed this advertisement. "George Frederick Handel (1685-1759), known for his swings from depression to mania, composed his majestic Messiah Oratorio in only six weeks. If he were living today, lithium would probably control his symptoms and he would give us his deathless, Bye Bye Blues."

~

Eh, there's trouble i' this world, and there's things we can niver make out the rights on. And all as we've got to do is to trusten, Master Marner— to do the right thing as far as we know and to trusten. For if us, as knows so little, can see a bit o' good and rights, we may be sure there's a good and a rights bigger nor what we can know— I feel it i' my own inside as it must be so.

—*Dolly Winthrop* in *Silas Marner.*

~

A woman who suffered great physical pain said, "I know God loves me, but I think an angel must have lost my file." —*Anonymous.*

~

When John Bright sat mourning in his widowed home, the economist, Richard Cobden, came to comfort him: "Bright," he said, "there are thousands of homes in England at this moment where wives, mothers, and children are dying of hunger. When the first pains of your grief are past, I would advise you to come with me and we will never rest until the Corn Laws are repealed."

~

"The room was dawn quiet. We all sat there, not knowing what to expect. Nothing moved; not even eyelashes flicked. Then, after eons of time, he came forward. Tiny droplets of perspiration appeared on his lineless face. After another interminable space of time, he raised his arms; his brows furrowed into contorted rivers; his skin darkened to deep vermillion from apparent inhuman exertion; the veins in his neck stood out like twisted rope. A look of intense pain racked his face. His eyes closed tight, the lids compressed to a thin line; his breathing was pained and intermittent. Finally, he looked up, relaxed a little and stared at us with pleading eyes. I felt a tremendous surge of sympathy and compassion for him. I spoke—though the emotion almost cut off my breath— 'That'spretty good harmonica playing for a ten year old!'" —*Robert Tinsley.*

~

The great Russian writer Andreev tells of the events of the crucifixion as seen through the eyes of a character, Ben Tovit. On the day that the Lord was killed, Ben Tovit was able to grasp only one thing and that was he had a toothache.

Occasionally he would catch a glimpse of a death procession wherein one was whipped as he carried a heavy cross through the streets. Later, there was the flash of a figure on a cross outlined against the sky but that was all he saw because Ben Tovit had a toothache.

~

How many people have lost their sight and gained 20/20 insight?
—*William Sloane Coffin.*

~

A deformed cripple and a hopeless beggar passed the holy man in prayer. The holy man asked God, "How can a loving creator see such folk and do nothing about it?" And God said, "I've done something about it. I made you." —*Sufi tale.*

~

It's remarkable with what Christian fortitude and resignation we can bear the suffering of other folks. —*Jonathan Swift.*

~

How did the golf ball get its dimples? When golf balls were first made they had smooth covers. Then it was discovered one got more distance from a ball that had been scarred. That's why they have dimples. —*Anonymous.*

~

How'd you get that wooden leg, sailor?
Oh, it was bit off by a shark. I almost drowned waiting to be rescued.
Phew! What a story; and how about that metal hook on your arm?
Yeah—I lost my arm in a sword fight. The coward snuck up behind me
        and cut off my hand—I had to finish him off with my other hand.
Wow! Is your eye patch from the same fight?
No, that was later. I got some dust in my eye.
You mean a tough guy like you lost an eye to a speck of dust?
Well—yeah. You see—that was the first day I got my hook.

~

Misery no longer loves company. Nowadays, it insists upon it. —*Russell Baker.*

~

Jesus Christ is always on the side of the crucified, and I believe he changes sides in the twinkling of an eye. He is not loyal to the person, or even less to the group; he is loyal to suffering. —*Peter Dumitriu.*

~

About catastrophe and how to behave in one, I know nothing—except what everyone else knows: If there when Grace dances, I should dance. —*W.H. Auden.*

~

Whenever pain is so borne as to be prevented from breeding bitterness, or any other evil fruit, a contribution is made to rescuing God's creation from the Devil's grip.—*The Doctrine of Atonement.*

~

James Atwood

TALENT

New York attracts the most talented people in the world in the arts and professions. In New York even the bums are talented.--Edmund Love, Subways Are for Sleeping.

~

You have to have a talent for having talent.
—*Ruth Gordon.*

~

A young composer came to Mozart for advice on how to develop creativity. "Begin writing simple things first—songs, for example," Mozart told the fellow. "But you composed symphonies when you were only a child," the man said. "Yes," replied Mozart, "but I didn't ask anyone to help me compose them!" —*Unknown.*

~

A little boy called his Dad out into the yard to show him how far he could hit a baseball. He tossed the ball in the air and took a mighty swing and missed. "Strike One," he said cheerily. He tried a second time, and missed again. "Strike Two," he called. Once more he threw it up and swung with all his might, but missed. "Strike three—I'm out," he said shrugging his shoulders. Then tucking his bat under his arm he looked up at his Dad and said, "Dad, I'm going to make a terrific pitcher."
—*Hoover Rupert, "Presbyterian Outlook".*

~

It was a rank amateur who built the ark. It was professionals who built the Titanic.

~

Martin Marty tells of a young man who rented a yacht on Sunday afternoons on Long Island Sound. He bought the cap, the map, and compasses, and talked a good line. Then his Jewish mother asked him, "By you, son, you're a sea captain; by me, you're a sea captain; but by sea captains, are you a sea captain?"

~

God doesn't make Antonio Stradivarius violins without Antonio.
—*Antonio Stradavarius.*

~

I'm not the handyman type so when something goes wrong around my place I must call a repairman or a gracious neighbor who can give me a helping hand. I try not to abuse the privilege with my neighbors; but I've gained a real good friend by saying, "Johnny, I wonder if you could help me take a look at my lawn mower? I can't get the thing started." Johnny's gifts have helped me. Asking Johnny for help is how we became friends. I also found out Johnny, who has recently retired, really needs to be needed.

~

Can't act—Can't sing—Slightly bald—Can dance a little.
—*Report of Fred Astaire's first screen test.*

102

When Sugar Ray Leonard spoke to the students at Harvard, he shared this wisdom:

I consider myself blessed. I consider you blessed.
We've all been blessed with God-given talents.
Mine just happens to be beatin' people up.
—*"Sports Illustrated".*

~

There are two kinds of talents; man-made talent and God-given talent. With man-made talent, you have to work very hard. With God-given talent, you just touch it up once in a while. —*Pearl Bailey.*

~

I have no voice for singing; I cannot make a speech;
I have no gift for music, I know I cannot teach.
I am no good at leading; I cannot organize.
And anything I write, would never win a prize.
It seems my only talent is neither large nor rare;
I just listen and encourage and fill a vacant chair.
—*Anonymous*

~

It took me fifteen years to discover I had no talent for writing, but I couldn't give it up because by that time I was too famous. —*Robert Benchley.*

~

If you want a track team to win the high jump, you find one person who can jump seven feet, not seven people who can jump one foot.
—*Frederick Terman, Provost, Stanford University.*

~

Back in the 40's, a well-known speaker was driving near Sing Sing Prison when a man at a stoplight asked him for a ride. As they were driving along he learned that the man had just been released from the prison. "What were you in for?" he asked. "For picking pockets," was the reply. The driver began to feel a bit uneasy—wondering how safe his watch and wallet and other valuables were. He didn't know what to do—so he decided to drive fast through small towns to attract a policeman's attention. Sure enough one pulled him over. He got out of the car, but so did the pickpocket. And he began to feel sorry for his passenger—after all—he had paid his debt to society. The officer wrote the speaker up a ticket and said, "You must appear before the judge tomorrow." The driver protested, "But, Officer, I have to give a speech in a town 300 miles away." That didn't make any difference to the officer. He just kept on writing his name and address in his little book. As they drove away he said to the pickpocket, "Just my luck! Having to appear before the judge ruins my whole schedule." The pickpocket asked, "Why do you have to show up in court, anyway?" The speaker replied, "The policeman's got my name and address, that's why." The pickpocket told him, "Not any more he don't. I've got his book." —*"Newsletter, Northeastern Retail Lumberman's Association", (1940).*

James Atwood

> *I had an old dog who was blue.*
> *But we called the old dog, 'Old Yeller.'*
> *The reason we called him, 'Old Yeller,'*
> *Is because he didn't have a stellar smeller.*
> — *Anonymous*

~

Albert Einstein was four before he could speak and seven before he could read. Isaac Newton was a poor student in Grade School. Walt Disney was fired as a newspaper editor because he didn't have any good ideas. Werner Van Braun failed algebra in the ninth grade. Haydn quit trying to make a musician out of Beethoven because he was too plodding a person and showed no talent.

--Alex McGinnis, Bringing Out The Best In People.

~

Use what talents you possess: the woods would be very silent if no birds sang there except those that sang best. — *Henry Van Dyke.*

~

When boxing legend, Joe Louis, was in the army, he and a friend were involved in a minor traffic accident. The other driver got out cursing and yelling, but Louis just stood there silently. Afterwards, the friend said, "Joe, why didn't you just knock him flat and shut him up for good?" Louis responded, "Why should I? When somebody insulted Caruso, did he sing for him?"

~

It takes little talent to see what lies under one's nose, but a good deal of it to know in what direction to point that organ. — *W.H. Auden.*

~

In 1722, the Town Council of Leipzig, Germany was looking for a new music teacher and organist for St. Thomas Church. The first person they selected turned them down, as did their second choice. One member of the Council expressed the sentiments of the group. "Since the best man cannot be obtained, we will have to accept a mediocre one." Their third choice was Johann Sebastian Bach.

~

God doesn't call the qualified. God qualifies the called — *Anonymous.*

~

To be a Christian does not mean to be religious in a particular way, to cultivate some particular form of asceticism (as a sinner, a penitent, or a saint), but to be a man. It is not some religious act that makes a Christian what he is, but participation in the suffering of God in the life of the world. It is only by living completely in this world that one learns to believe. One must abandon every attempt to make something of oneself, whether it be a saint, a converted sinner, a churchman, a righteous man or an unrighteous one, a sick man or a healthy one. This is what I mean by worldliness—taking life in one's stride, with all its duties and problems, its successes and failures, its experiences and helplessness.

--Dietrich Bonhoeffer, Letters and Papers from Prison.

~

TEMPTATION

"

Despite a severely tight budget, the wife of a seminary student bought hersrelf an expensive Easter dress. Her husband fussed at her. "When you were tempted to buy it, you should have said, "Get thee behind me, Satan." Thoughfully, the wife responded, "Well, Dear—that's exactly what I did say, and Satan whispered to me that it looked good from the rear!" — *David MacLennan, Church Chuckles.*

~

When the youth group visited a coal mine, one of the girls wore a white dress. She asked the miner who was to be their guide, "Can't I wear a white dress into the mine?" The miner answered hesitatingly, "Yes, young lady, you certainly can wear a white dress into the mine, but you won't wear a white dress back."

~

Most people who flee temptation leave their forwarding address. — *Anonymous.*

~

Admiral Byrd and his staff were reflecting on the things they missed the most while stationed at the South Pole. Byrd turned to one man who wasn't saying much and asked him what he missed most? "Temptation," he sighed.

~

If the apple had been a brussels sprout, we'd all still be in paradise!

~

One hears, till one is weary, about the temptations of New York City. With joy I celebrate the temptations of New York City: temptations to music, to art, to social service, to the support of interracial goodwill and international concord. Here, where the currents of the world flow through, how can men and women live thinking only of temptations downward when there are so many alluring temptations upward?" —*Harry Emerson Fosdick.*

~

Have you ever heard of a blind nudist? A one-eyed nudist?

~

There are several good protections against temptation, but the surest is cowardice.
—*Mark Twain.*

~

Things forbidden have a secret charm. —*Tacitus.*

~

I generally avoid temptation unless I can't resist it. —*Mae West.*

~

A father told his son about the sheep who found a hole in the fence and slipped through and played in the open fields until dark; but then it could not find its way home again, and a wolf that chased it until the shepherd rescued it, carrying it back to the fold. The boy asked, "Daddy, did the shepherd fix the hole in the fence?"

~

Opportunity knocks only once; temptation bangs on your door forever.

~

A minister parked his car in a no-parking zone in Philadelphia and attached a note to his windshield: "I have circled this block ten times. I have an appointment to keep. Forgive us our trespasses." When he returned, he found this reply along with a ticket. "I've circled this block for 10 years. If I don't give you a ticket, I lose my job. Lead us not into temptation."

~

Don't worry about avoiding temptation. As you grow older, it will avoid you.
—*Winston Churchill.*

~

Dishonesty is never an accident. Good people never see temptation when they meet it. —*English proverb.*

~

Ever notice that the whisper of temptation can be heard farther than the loudest call to duty? —*Earl Wilson.*

~

After starting a new diet, I altered my drive to work to avoid passing my favorite bakery. I accidentally drove by the bakery one morning and there in the window was a host of goodies. I felt this was no accident, so I prayed, "God, it's up to you if you want me to have any of those delicious goodies, create a parking place for me directly in front of the bakery." And sure enough, God answered my prayer. On the eighth time around the block—there it was!

~

VICTORY

Don't wait until the battle is over. Shout now!

~

A cornerback for the Washington Redskins was congratulated after winning a large contract. "You are the luckiest guy I know," said his teammate, "You get more good contracts and endorsements than anyone I know." He didn't consider it luck. He was in the weight room and on the practice field every day.

~

It's amazing how lucky you get when you're good! —*Tom Brookshire, Football announcer.*

~

The race is not always to the swift, nor the battle to the strong, but that's the way to bet!" —*Damon Runyan.*

~

Straight shooters always win.
—*Tom Mix.*

~

Walk cheerfully over the world. Sing and rejoice, Children of the Day and of the Light. —*George Fox, Quaker Leader, (17th C.).*

~

I feel sorry for someone who has to win at everything! —*Snoopy.*

It matters not whether you win or lose. What matters is whether I win or lose.--Unknown.

~

There are some defeats more triumphant than victories. —*Michel de Montaigne.*

~

Often the best way to win is to forget to keep score. —*Marianne Espinosa Murphy.*

~

In explaining his teams' record of two wins, seven losses and one tie, the coach said, "We overwhelmed two of our opponents, underwhelmed seven, and whelmed one."

~

A short summary of all Jewish holidays: *They tried to kill us, we won, let's eat.*
                                                                            --Unknown.

~

One of the best stories to come out of the struggle to end apartheid in South Africa was of Bishop Desmond Tutu staring down the South African Security Police who broke into a worship service at the cathedral . They had writing pads and tape recorders to capture any words to provide cause to jail the Bishop or worshipers who resisted their power. (A few weeks before, Tutu had been arrested and jailed.) Tutu stopped his sermon, looked right at the police and said, "You are powerful, very powerful. But we are here worshiping a higher power than you. We serve a God who cannot be mocked." Smiling, he continued, "Since you have already lost, I invite you today to come and join the winning side." Immediately, the whole congregation leaped to its feet, dancing. The police, dumbfounded, retreated before the worshipers, who danced out into the streets.

~

James Reston said of Reagan's Secretary of the Interior, James Watt, that he had the good judgment to quit while he was behind.

~

Two friends were having a heart-to-heart conversation. "My family was very poor, and I wasn't able to go to college. But I've learned over the years that a guy with guts and discipline can overcome hardships like that, even though I didn't."

~

Whenever someone would ask forlornly: "Where are our leaders today?" Lisa Sullivan, of The Children's Defense Fund, would get mad and say, "We are the ones we have been waiting for."

~

When the Brooklyn Dodgers won the World Series, Yogi Berra informed Al Campanis of the Dodgers front office, "You wouldn't have won if we had beaten you."

~

An aura of victory surrounds a person of good will.

~

ABOUT THE AUTHOR

Jim Atwood, a retired Presbyterian minister, was born in Detroit, but grew up in Florida, and has lived most of his life in the South. He graduated in physical education from Florida State University, holds Masters degrees from Union Theological Seminary in Richmond, VA, and Princeton Theological Seminary, and a Doctor of Ministry Degree from McCormick Theological Seminary.

First a son and student, then an athlete, a missionary and student worker in Japan, pastor to three congregations, and activist for peace and justice, he is also a grateful husband, proud father, doting grandfather, minister's spouse, and a sport's and travel addict—all rich grist for his humor mill.

Atwood serves on national boards for The Presbyterian Peace Fellowship and The Coalition to Stop Gun Violence.

ABOUT THE ILLUSTRATOR

Pat McGeachy is a writer, cartoonist, and retired Presbyterian Minister who lives in Nolensville, Tennessee. He has authored more than thirty books, including *The Gospel According to Andy Capp*; *Help, Lord*; and the *Folk Psalm Book*.

James Atwood

Blank Page

The Leaven of Laughter Series

WONDER WHAT'S AROUND
THE BEND

The Leaven of Laughter
> *For Advent and Christmas*

The Leaven of Laughter
> *About Being Human*

The Leaven of Laughter
> *It's All About Money*

The Leaven of Laughter
> *The Bible and Theology*

The Leaven of Laughter
> *From Arguments to Nuclear War*

The Leaven of Laughter
> *The Fruits of the Spirit and Other Virtues*

The Leaven of Laughter
> *The Works of the Flesh and Other Sins*

The Leaven of Laughter
> *The Work and Worship of the Church*

The Leaven of Laughter
> *Organized Religion (The Church as Organization)*